Listening to History

For my
Father and Mother
who left such rich memories
and for
Sylvia
who shares them with me.

Listening to History
The authenticity of oral evidence

Trevor Lummis

BARNES & NOBLE BOOKS
TOTOWA, NEW JERSEY

First published in the USA 1988 by
BARNES & NOBLE BOOKS
81 ADAMS DRIVE
TOTOWA, NEW JERSEY, 07512

© Trevor Lummis 1987

Set in 10/12pt Times by
D. P. Media Limited, Hitchin, Hertfordshire

Printed and bound in Great Britain by
Richard Clay Ltd, Bungay, Suffolk

Library of Congress Cataloging-in-Publication Data

Lummis, Trevor.
    Listening to history / Trevor Lummis.
        p. cm.
    Bibliography: p.
    Includes index.   27.50
    ISBN 0–389–20779–9
    1. Oral history. I. Title.
D16.14.L86 1988   87–35430
907'.2—dc19   CIP

ISBN: 0–389–20779–9

Contents

Preface

There is a history in all men's lives
Figuring the nature of the time deceased

William Shakespeare
Henry IV, Part 2

The main theme of this book is a consideration of the authenticity of oral evidence. The task of creating authentic information is present at every stage from interviewing an individual and understanding their personal account through to aggregating one specific item of information from each of hundreds of interviews in a large archive. What follows then is concerned with all aspects of the practice of oral history, from who and how to interview to the value of computerized indexing and the analysis of large archives. It is not, however, intended as an instruction manual – it does not discuss recording equipment nor give advice on how to set up an oral history project – but it is intended to be a guide to informed practice for those who wish to do fieldwork and for those who wish to use oral evidence only as a source of historical evidence generated by others. I believe that the desire to collect and interpret such information with maximum fidelity is of equal concern to the numerous people now involved in practising oral history, be they individuals, local history groups, undergraduates or professional historians. Anyone who sets out with a tape-recorder to collect historical information must intend to do so effectively and accurately; anyone who wishes only to use the results of such fieldwork needs to be aware of its strengths and weaknesses; and both will handle the material more effectively if they have thought through the method from beginning to end.

The shape of the following chapters was largely dictated by the sequence of generating oral history data, and the content was determined by those issues which have emerged from my experience of oral history reviewed in the light of general practice. Whatever may be the defects in the treatment which follows I am confident that the issues raised are crucial to oral history. In so far as oral history is now an indispensable source of historical evidence the issue of authenticity is also germane to historical methodology at large.

Part One   *Oral History, its Value and Definition*

1 Introduction

> Have no faith in history, look upon it as a mass of fabrications, concocted, like modern newspapers, not with any regard to truth, or the interests of humanity, but to deceive the multitude, and thus to bolster up all the frauds and villainous institutions of the rich.
>
> James Bronterre O'Brien
> *Poor Man's Guardian*, 5 December 1835

One hopes that history has improved since O'Brien wrote those words. Labour, feminist, family and a growing variety of working-class histories demonstrate that the multitude is now more widely represented in written history: and if the 'truth' of the more recent accounts is just as open to question at least there is a wider selection of 'frauds' from which to choose. Whether newspapers have undergone the same diversification or whether they still remain the 'villainous institutions of the rich' I will leave to common knowledge and the facts of ownership.

It may appear slightly perverse to start a book on oral history by citing the fallibility of a documentary source. But as critics of oral history so frequently contrast it to the assumed greater reliability of contemporary documentary evidence it is worth reminding ourselves that such sources also have their biases and distortions which, while acknowledged in books on methodology, are rarely allowed for in practice. Omissions are an even greater defect than errors, for much of historical interest is not recorded in any documentary source. The great advantage of the retrospective interview is that it enables historians to intervene directly in the generation of historical evidence relating to the recent past, and so it becomes possible for the historian to collect the type of evidence which customary documentary and material sources have not supplied. This is an inestimable asset as the value of any historical evidence is not entirely intrinsic but is affected by the amount and quality of the sources of similar evidence. Oral history should be a good deal more informative and precise than even various forms of autobiography and personal testimony simply because it is the product of two people (the informant and the researcher) and as such is focused more on historical than on biographical concerns.

There is no reason why those who use oral evidence should be on the defensive when faced with the issue of the respective value of documentary and oral sources. Documents are produced by institutions (villainous and otherwise) for their own purposes and historical study is rarely one of them. It would be beyond the scope of this book to discuss the defects of a great deal of documentary evidence. It is sufficient to note here that the various parliamentary inquiries into industrial conditions and social problems are often among the most useful documentary sources for social history. The verbatim evidence given to these inquiries is frequently indistinguishable from the sort of testimony given in an oral history interview; informants recall their working lives and conditions and what is recorded in these inquiries is often their *past* experience. The point does not need belabouring; much documentary evidence is oral evidence which has been committed to paper at a particular point in time. The problems of memory – how fallible it is and how biased retrospective evidence may be – which are attributed to oral evidence are actually an epistemological problem of much other historical evidence made visible and inescapable. Questions of authenticity raised in the specific context of oral evidence are pertinent to a much wider body of historical evidence as well as to the widespread use of the interview method in the social sciences.

This book is an attempt to address some of the main doubts about oral evidence as a source of historical knowledge and, more constructively, to consider what practices might improve the quality of oral evidence. Many doubts are more or less closely tied to the nature of memory and whether the past can be remembered as a mirror image or is reshaped and reconstructed through time as we grow to have new values, attitudes and perspectives on our lives, and as social values and practices change. Does memory suppress relevant experience as some psychological theorists claim, or do we simply forget whole chunks of experience, so reporting a part as the whole with all the distortions that would imply? At another level do people attempt to tell the truth about the past even if they can remember it? Doubts can range from the common-sense evaluation of some informants as telling tall tales through to theoretical perspectives which claim that pristine memory of the past does not exist and that there is only present consciousness. But whether there are pure memories, distorted memories or only present consciousness, the fact remains that people believe that they have memories, that they are a source of information and that that information requires serious evaluation. Other issues common to anyone using oral evidence concern the degree to which material from a single life history can provide evidence of wider historical changes, how typical this single account of its time and place can be, and whether the experience of a few interviews can form the basis of a general social interpretation. One might even ask why we are doing this, what is its purpose?

These questions should also be asked of documentary evidence but seldom are. Because they are contemporary, documents give a certain specious air of being trustworthy accounts of that period. But history does not happen in documents. Human activity happens as lived experience before being set down by some individual (often on behalf of an organization) and is to that extent retrospective and secondhand. Even reports of what a witness said in court are hardly contemporary evidence given the law's delay. The biases some fear in retrospective oral evidence can be far less evident than those in contemporary statements. An account of an infringement of the law at the time is probably less true than an account given twenty years later when the consequences of the truth are no longer unpleasant. This can be repeated in less extreme and obvious areas: truth is rarely maximized by being close to any event.

The practice of oral history has had the important, if unforeseen, effect of revitalizing debates on common-sense interpretation, methodology and theoretical formation which lie behind the interpretation of most forms of historical evidence. The debate on oral evidence is particularly valuable because it brings into sharp focus a number of issues of wider historical methodology. Oral history has in addition raised issues about the purpose of history. As one goes to a community or group to collect evidence, evidence which contains *their* interpretation of their life and events, one is particularly conscious of the cooperative basis of the project. This raises direct questions on the historians' moral and political responsibility to the people they write about. They are not just shadows from the far past, mere names on documents, but people who have invited one into their homes, provided hospitality and given of their time and memories. But, once again, if historians should respect their contact with this generation they should also respect earlier ones.

The political aspects of oral history have exercised many. This is, as I see it, because in the past the 'silence' of the great under-privileged mass of workers was explained through their lack of access to the making of the historical record. The failure of workers to be militant could be explained through the incorporation of their leaders into the existing power structure and political system. But once oral evidence became widely available through tape-recordings, the fact that the majority of those interviewed expressed only low levels of resentment to their employers or to the police or other institutions of social control was disconcerting for some poli-tical activists – and many good social historians are both activists and socialists – because the lack of militancy seemed to throw the Marxian potential of the working class into some doubt. On the other hand, if memory can be shown to be defective or selective in providing a 'Golden Age' view of the past then theories of class resentment and resistance are not affected. If memory can be equated with present consciousness then the lack of past militancy can be explained as the control of the historical images by the present distribution of class power, as succinctly expressed by Orwell's dictum 'He who controls the present controls the past, he who controls the past controls the future'. These issues are crucial to the authenticity of the historical content of oral accounts.

In addition to these issues there are a number of more arcane debates about language, symbols and myth which concern oral history because it is a process of communication. Ultimately these issues will have a bearing on the interpretation of oral history but I do not discuss them here. This is due partly to my limited grasp of the subject-matter, and partly to the fact that the issues they raise are relevant to all forms of communication and therefore not ger-mane to oral history in particular: as the substance of those debates enters into general discourse so they will also enter the realm of oral history. In other words it is a question of priority. It may be a moot point whether contemporary speech can delineate aspects of the real world of either the past or present, but it is one that we have to take for granted.

In selecting the content for discussion I have been guided by those issues which seem to me most directly relevant, useful and informa-tive to those who want to practise or use oral evidence.[1]* In present-ing the arguments I have been influenced by my perception of how

* Superior figures refer to the Notes at the end of the main text.

most people will approach the subject: that is by collecting the evidence, then analysing and using it and through this process coming to question its validity, think about its problems and how they can present it.

The discussion is divided into three parts. Part One defines oral history and describes its development. Part Two is about the choice of informants, the importance of a questionnaire and the interview. Part Three examines, first, how to evaluate the authenticity of a single interview by using internal consistency and external evaluators, and second, how aggregating the data in a number of interviews can be used to assess their typicality and to provide some grounds upon which to build generalizations. The aim throughout is to emphasize that each step in the process can improve the final value of reminiscences as historical information. These sections do not require a lengthy introduction as their sequence and purpose is largely self-evident. It may be appropriate to note here that methodological aspects – such as 'sampling' or 'interviewer bias' – are discussed only in so far as they are 1 levant to oral history, although I trust that the various references will be an adequate guide to those who may wish to pursue any of these aspects in greater detail.

The serial nature of print and of argument compel one to take the subject a chapter at a time and that, of course, somewhat over-schematizes and sets apart subjects which need to be considered in relation to each other. This text is conceived very much as a whole in which one part will not reveal its full meaning until all parts have been read. For example, Part Two depends upon the practices advocated in Part One for much of its validity, just as the confident positivistic methology of that part is later tempered by other perspectives presented in Part Four. The uniting element is precisely my belief that authenticity cannot suddenly be divined in an interview but that achieving authenticity has to be part of the entire practice from conceiving an interview through to the archiving of a whole collection of them. By 'authenticity' I mean the best account that it is possible to achieve by self-conscious methodology. Questions of 'truth' and of the relationship between 'reality' and 'appearances' – although of great interest to historians along with everyone else – are matters of philosophy: to discuss them here would be to write a different book.

2 Origins and potential

The bias it [oral history] introduces into history is wholly welcome because it will necessarily direct the historian's attention to the fundamental common things of life: the elements of individual and social experience rather than upon administrative and political chronologies. It makes it possible for the historian to define his subject in the same way as the sociologist or the social anthropologist, and to pick his themes before he starts in the light of their substantive importance, rather than to leave himself at the mercy of his documents, following them more or less compulsively because there is no other evidence on which he can draw. The reason why history has so often a bureaucratic bias is not I think because of the particular bias of individual historians, but very largely because bureaucratic documents are the ones most often preserved.

R. Samuel
Oral History, **1**, no. 4, 1973, pp. 119–20

At least since the time of the Ancient Greeks historians have asked participants in past events to communicate their memories as part of the historical record. These have been most frequently the memories and opinions of great men. It is not my intention to review the historical development of oral evidence as this has been done at length elsewhere.[1] It is sufficient for our purposes to note that some of the first recordings were made by folklorists in the late nineteenth century who, under the influence of romantic nationalism, were interested in ensuring the survival of the traditional, rural and demotic. In the 1920s the Chicago School of sociology used life histories as a means of investigating contemporary society, especially the world of outsiders, deviants and criminals. The crucial point here is the understanding gained from listening to the informants' accounts of causes and motivation rather than the interpretations of social workers, medical practitioners, law officers and enforcement agencies. Although these accounts were collected as part of a contemporary sociological and political concern they relied on retrospective recall as they looked at social processes through the informants' own life experiences.

What these precursors had in common was that the inquiry's focus was usually on the ordinary person, particularly the working class and underprivileged. This gave modern oral history a prime interest in those classes and groups in society which, although part of a literate society and often literate themselves, did not leave much documentary evidence of their own creation. If documented at all they appeared either through the official records of the state or through the eyes of their middle-class and upper-class contemporaries. Relative economic, social and political power effects the access particular groups have to the production and the preservation of documentary sources of all types. Giving a voice to the voiceless has been a strong impulse in the development of oral history. The area of interest has since widened from the rural and traditional or the deviant to include the urban working class and minority groups, although it is equally useful for shedding historical light on any social group.

Oral history in its present form permits the purposeful intervention of historians in collecting the data needed to illuminate particular areas about which too little information has survived from other sources. It is an ideal method for studying the recent past of unorganized workers, domestic life, attitudes and ideology at the grassroots, the experience of childhood or indeed any historical dimension which can be explored through lived experience. In Europe, for example, it is now virtually the only method of fully exploring the many underground struggles against fascism because these were by definition clandestine and often undocumented by those involved.[2]

Given such precursors, it is rather ironic that modern oral history started in 1948 at Columbia University with Allan Nevins recording 'significant' Americans. His purpose was to use oral history to fill a noticeable gap in the level of personal documentation generated by prominent people who no longer wrote letters or kept diaries on the scale of their nineteenth-century counterparts. Initially the oral communication was seen merely as a means of producing a document. Although American oral history started as a study of elites, it soon returned to its folkloric and sociological roots and in the late 1960s diversified as a history of non-elite groups, sharing the main focus of most European oral history. And although elite groups are still researched, the study of non-elites is now central to oral history throughout the world.

Interview material is now such an important source that it is difficult to visualize a rounded social history without it. The history of working-class domestic life, for example, appears in the records mainly from the observations (and through the values) of law-enforcement agencies, social workers or similar semi-official bodies whose main contacts were with the unfortunate minority who were obliged to recourse to charities and the state. Even the domestic life of the upper and middle classes is over-represented by the large estates which kept household accounts, farm books, game books, menus, guest lists and so forth. These are supplemented by auto-biographies, letters and diaries (which tend to over-represent the literary and political elites) as well as portraits and household artifacts of all kinds. Little was documented or owned by the working class; most of the few documents were destroyed and most of the artifacts worn out: cramped working-class homes were not designed to accommodate even one generation very satisfactorily, much less the past of a previous one. But even amongst the elite the documentary survivals are mainly of particular types and oral evidence is still a useful addition to their record.

But the importance of oral evidence to history does not rely entirely, or even mainly, on its ability to create sources for the understanding of unrepresented groups; it provides the basis for considering a much wider range of historical questions. For example, the development of labour and working-class history has been dominated by the study of political organizations and trade unions. But only a minority were members of a party or union, so accounts written solely from such sources can only be a partial account of a particular group of males, and the institutional focus ensured that the history of women would be virtually ignored. The feminist movement has made women visible in many areas of history by re-examining existing evidence, but for the recent past oral evidence has extended the range of subjects which can be investigated as well as the depth and strength of the conclusions. Above all oral evidence gives us the opportunity to understand the history of the people rather than of activists, leaders of people or their formal organizations. One will never gain a rounded picture of industrial conditions from the records of either trade unions or employers. Each is making a case for either more or fewer hours of work and levels of pay. Each discusses the issue at the level of the formal and legal. The actual story lies at the informal level where the real intensity of work, the amount of perks to be had and the actual degree of managerial control are all germane to a fuller understanding of industrial and social relations. Above all oral evidence is dynamic. It allows the previous domestic background, social attitudes, political views, leisure activities – indeed, virtually any dimension of a person's prior experience which may be thought to have shaped their expectations – to be considered. So we are not presented with a static snapshot of certain conditions co-existing with certain attitudes and values, but rather with their historical development.

Another advantage of oral evidence is that it can be created by historians. They can decide what evidence they require. It is, then, a particularly challenging type of history for which there are few excuses for failure: lack of the right type of evidence, paucity of records and so on are the constant reason and excuse for the limitations of historical writing. To come face to face with the participants in events, and to be able to ask them what one will, challenges the historical imagination. Not only do oral historians have a challenge in terms of their own research interests; they have a responsibility to create information of general historical interest. Faced with an informant who occupied a particular historical and social location one should interview with an eye to future scholarship and maximize the value of the contribution informants are willing to make.

Not that oral history is a preserve of professional historians. Oral history can be practised by the layman armed with nothing more than a tape-recorder and genuine historical curiosity. At the personal level of family history a cassette of our grandparents relating their lives will be far more fascinating to our grandchildren and great grandchildren than a name on a geneaological tree. Indeed, elderly relatives can often furnish the married names and family histories of unknown great-aunts or more distant relatives, and as finding and cross-linking documentary information is often one of the more difficult aspects of historical work even one interview can be an invaluable guide. Being *told* who aunts and uncles were and the maiden names of female relatives by marriage, their occupations, and what is recalled of their life is much easier and more productive than trying to establish these from documentary sources. It can save an enormous amount of time to discuss family history with elderly relatives before attempting to approach the records of state and church. Indeed, even one interview with a neighbour or ex-workmate will probably yield more information about a deceased and hitherto unknown relative than all the documents to be found.

Oral history's role in giving a voice to underprivileged sectors of society whose lives appear in the historical record largely through the eyes, prejudices and testimony of their social superiors, leads many oral historians to assume that it is essentially democratic and radical. They are, I believe, in error: the method is at best neutral and, used carelessly, overwhelmingly conservative. Most people show an amazing resilience to, and even create pleasures amongst, the most appalling circumstances of deprivation. In interviews which reveal that the informants were worked intensively for long hours, at wages which were too inadequate to satisfy even the basic needs for food and shelter, much less furnish the means by which to develop their innate capacities, informants will still relate the pleasures and satisfactions of their lives. This is not necessarily a retrospective bias or selective memory causing them to forget the bad times and remember only the good – as most people remember only the sunny days of childhood summers. People are obliged to live their lives in whatever circumstances they find themselves and that is a process of psychological as well as physical survival. If some achieved this through active struggle, either for the general better-ment of their class or as an individual aspiration to rise to the next class, the majority simply accepted the circumstances and adapted their expectations to what was available. They extracted much fun from small pleasures and deep satisfactions from modest achieve-ments and possessions. It is difficult to go through life, to continue it, if there are no pleasures; even the immates of prison camps find occasions for humour. The vast majority of people live in the community into which history and chance has precipitated them and make the best of it. Because oral history accounts relate the pleasures and satisfactions of life alongside the meagre material conditions, there is a real danger of perpetuating the 'poor but happy' image of life which is, paradoxically, used to justify the comfortable in the enjoyment of their more ample possessions.

3 Definition

> . . . in oral history the aim is to gain information about the past; in the biographical life history, to gain information about a person's development; and in the sociological life history, to grasp the ways in which a particular person constructs and makes sense of his or her life at a given moment. The goal of life history analysis will dramatically affect issues of validity. For instance, the oral historian's goal – of recapturing the past – is altogether more ambitious than the sociologist's, . . .

> Ken Plummer
> *Documents of Life*, No. 7 of Contemporary Social Research Series, General Editor M. Bulmer (George Allen & Unwin 1983), p. 105

To attempt to recapture the past through oral evidence is an ambitious goal: history is ambitious in that it is trying to reconstruct and understand societies from the material traces they leave behind. The previous chapter has argued that given the inadequacy of other sources, oral evidence stands alone as the only major resource for large areas of experience. But as Plummer points out above, interviewing someone about their life can be carried out for different purposes and this implies a different level of authenticity according to the use made of the evidence. So although defining any subject can be a stultifying process if it is intended to draw boundaries and include in the ranks of practitioners only those who can meet the demands of rigorously-drawn criteria (and that is far from the intention here), an attempt to define essential elements is useful to all concerned in its practice because it focuses attention on what is central to the activity and what is peripheral, what improves the authenticity of the testimony and what does not.

As with many developing activities a definitive formula for oral history practice has not emerged, although Willa K. Baum has written how at the American Oral History Association's first meeting '. . . the definition of oral history was roundly debated. No exact boundaries have ever been agreed upon, nor should they be, . . .' but then continues by suggesting that every interviewer should feel an obligation to other scholars and posterity by gathering as broad a range of information as possible, that the discussion should be by question and answer with an informed interviewer, and that the record '. . . be taken down as completely and accurately as possible, this being much aided by the tape recorder'.[1] We might start from her rather broad point about responsibility to posterity if only because it does distinguish one aspect of interviewing for oral history purposes from other aspects of life history interviewing. We are not simply collecting contemporary or psychological information about the present state of our informants, but attempting to collect information about the past. Not only does historical evidence become more useful when it can be placed into context, but while we have the opportunity of interviewing for our own interests it takes only a little more effort to include in the conversation subjects of interest to other historians. In other words oral history is not simply biographical or personal in intent however much it resembles those at the moment of generation. The degree to which, and how widely, that information can contribute to the historical record and present and future analysis is part of the professional responsibility of good practice.

Willa Baum's inclusion of the question and answer format seems a little formal at first glance, but it serves to draw a distinction between oral history and the self-recorded autobiographical monologue or reminiscence. Once again this is not to say that such solitary ventures are not worthwhile – the historical record would be richer had more people recorded themselves. But part of the advantage of the oral history method lies in the active intervention by a researcher in the recording of an individual's experience. It is this which should ensure that a testimony which is uniquely valuable in itself gains added value by contributing its information and insights to a systematic collection of material. If oral history is a method at all it must include an element of pre-planning, a prior interest in certain historical and intellectual problems, or, at the very least, an awareness of gaps in the evidence which oral history is attempting to fill. It is unreasonable to expect every person who is willing to record their experiences to know which aspects of their experience will be of interest to the historical record – and if researchers are no more omniscient at least two heads are better than one.

Many practitioners of oral history have shown a great deal of ambivalence about the need for an informed interviewer. Some of the reasons for this are dealt with later in this book. Briefly, it is related to the ideal of oral history as something ordinary people can do for themselves: an activity which is intellectually, socially and politically democratic and collective. Much depends on the purpose of the research. For example, if one was interviewing cabinet ministers, high civil servants and similar elite personages about a history of a particular political policy, very little would be liable to emerge unless one was thoroughly informed on the likely role of various personalities, the sequence of events, and had a detailed knowledge of the workings of the political and governmental machine. Knowledge of any area of experience about which one is interviewing can be a tremendous advantage in ensuring that the conversation is pursued intelligently and in knowing where to question and deepen an informant's account. Many wish to avoid the conclusion that the interviewer needs to be well informed, however, because this would imply that oral history is restricted to an informed elite and/or professional historians. They would argue that a genuine historical curiosity and the ability to listen are an interviewer's most important assets; and that oral history can be collected by the layman with very little experience or knowledge because, after all, it is the informants' experience and knowledge which are the essential elements. As a person recording their memories alone is better than no memoirs, so I would argue that oral history done by people with no special expertise is better than no oral history at all. That said, I cannot doubt that oral evidence collected within the framework of certain methodological guidelines and an informed historical imagination is a more useful and better historical source than ill-informed practice. One solution to the problem of varying levels of expertise lies with the considerable number of local history groups who undertake oral history as a collective enterprise in which expertise, insights and practical experience are pooled in a group activity.

The importance of the level of expertise is partially mitigated where the interviews are recorded and the tapes preserved, so that subsequent users of the material can listen to the exchange and evaluate for themselves the value of the interview. I would go much further than that earlier suggestion of the American Oral History Association that it is merely 'desirable' that the information be taken down by a tape-recorder: for my part tape-recording (or other method of recording sound) is an essential part of the method and should be included in the definition. An interview should be on a system of reproducible sound so preserving the spoken word as the original historical source. Oral history is a methodology, not a historical sub-field such as political, economic or social history, so although it can contribute information to all those fields the contribution depends upon the authenticity of the source, and this is best guaranteed by the rigour of the method. Oral communication is different in kind from written sources: it is richer in communicative power, containing as it does, inflections, hesitations, expressions and nuances not reproducible in written form. Both the oral and aural quality of the historical source may be thought of as part of its distinguishing feature. Recording interviews and preserving the tapes as the original source is necessary to establish the provenance and authenticity of the evidence. Transcriptions of the recordings may be thought adequate enough to contain all the historical information, but once the recording is erased there is no certain proof that the transcription is either full or correct. If a recording is destroyed after a typescript has been made we are left with a documentary source of a certain claimed provenance, which nevertheless is a copy with the possibility of error and omissions.

Where the original conversation was not recorded the information has different epistemological status: it becomes hearsay evidence. This has a proper historical use and is sometimes the only evidence available for an event, but it must be appreciated that it has a degree of 'reality' which is different from a firsthand account from the actual witness to events. Yet a study of elite oral historians (those historians whose informants and subjects of study are predominantly public figures) defines oral history as 'remembered conversation': a definition that is far too loose to be useful. That definition emerged from a survey of seventy-five elite historians and authors, fifty-five of whom replied to a questionnaire. 'Approximately 60 per cent of the respondents in the survey preferred to take notes, but a significant 18 per cent preferred tape recording (the remaining 22 per cent relied on memory and subsequently wrote up notes).'[2] This is not the place to review all the objections to the fallibility of remembered conversations, and the danger of errors of understanding which occur in note-taking in the field. The simple positive point is that *a recording establishes beyond doubt what was said by whom and with what expression.* Even a simple word like 'Yes' can be stated instantly and decisively in response to a query or in a hesitant drawl, as if to signify that it is only marginally more accurate than 'No'. A recording not only preserves this evidence in which the tone is as revealing as the word, but gives proof of whether the researcher followed-up this hesitancy by exploring the subject further or accepted it at its face value. Thus a recording is a record not simply of the content but also of the research process itself, and that can reveal the most likely areas of omissions, misunderstandings and biases. Even Antony Seldon, who used the definition 'remembered conversation', expresses a preference for the value of the tape because it records all, is accurate and therefore of more use to future historians; researchers' notes are just notes of aspects which were important to them, whereas a recorded conversation inevitably contains much information not relevant to one's own interests but which can prove invaluable to the historical record.

In defining oral history we are concerned only to establish the authenticity of recorded information, not hearsay or various combinations of note-taking in the field or writing-up in retrospect which leave the actual words and evidence of the informant available only at secondhand – although such notes and observations can be a valuable addition to an interview. One also has to acknowledge that elite oral history is an especially difficult genre in that one is interviewing people with public reputations, departmental loyalties, and political allegiances to defend and uphold. As part of a governing elite they are very self-conscious and aware of just how what they say might be used to their own or their colleagues' discredit. Perhaps these difficulties seriously affect the quality of oral evidence available from this group, but whatever the reasons, the practice of the majority of elite scholars does not advance the use of oral evidence as an authentic source based on recognized methodology open to improvement by thought and practice.

However we define oral history, it has obvious affinities with 'life history' – in fact oral history interviewing is sometimes loosely referred to as the life history method. There are distinctions, however, which help to delineate more precisely what is central to oral history. The difference between the way social scientists use life story methodology and oral history is one of central focus: life story emphasis is on the subjective world of the informant (although that is understood within the structures of history and sociology), whereas oral history is primarily concerned with gathering information about historical and social structures (although the person's subjectivity will be apparent and of interest at the same time). This difference of focus has significant repercussions for the way in which information can be used with confidence. Unless oral historians can collect useful information about the past, as opposed to present states of mind, then the argument for practising oral history largely disappears.

If oral history is definitionally distinct from life history because of its concern with the past rather than present consciousness, then it also needs to be separated from 'Oral Tradition' because oral tradition's major focus is on the past beyond the recall of one lifespan. The term 'oral tradition' is normally applied to the practice of those historians working on the history of non-literate societies. This is a very difficult area of historical work where the oral traditions of a people are used to reconstruct their chronology, migrations, political and cultural history. The means by which this is done varies with the sources available; but many cultures have professional remembrancers who are trained to remember by rote aspects of the history of their people; some may specialize, for example, in remembering the geneaology of the ruling household, others the laws of society or the historical accounts which embody claims to, or indicate the previous extent of, their tribal possessions. Other oral traditions are less consciously preserved and are related more as entertainment, whose content nevertheless reveals much about the values and *mores* of society. What is distinctive about this information is that it is what someone has been told and is not about their personal experience. The process of transmission from generation to generation presents problems of validity which do not apply to memories of direct experiences, which is the central subject matter of oral history.[3] Oral history interviews will collect a certain amount of information of this sort, such as folk songs and tales, myths and specific collective interpretations of the past. More common are accounts that the parents or grandparents of the informants have given them about their own experience. Once again this information is valuable and revealing but it is essential to appreciate that it has a relation to reality which is different from accounts of direct experience. They are remembered anecdotes, isolated incidents and 'facts' which often cannot be placed in the context of the rest of a person's life in the same way that 'facts' of direct experience can. These accounts by parents and grandparents were often told when the informant was a child and they may have misunderstood or forgotten essential elements. Nevertheless, even where such information may not be factually true, though accurately transmitted and remembered, it can be a valuable indication of values and attitudes within the family. Evidence does not have to be literally 'true' in order to be of historical value, myths are potent determinants of belief and activity, and some of these stories of their forbears' doings may have the status of moral precepts which shape behaviour. It is important, however, to be able to distinguish between fact and fiction, not to reject one or other, but in order to evaluate and use the evidence to better purpose.

My final definitional point would be that oral history is retrospective. There have been 'oral history' projects recording the course of contemporary political and industrial events, with the aim of anticipating what kind of information historians will need and recording it at the time. Such activities will undoubtedly be of immense value to historians in the future, but only as a contemporary document or recording. 'History' is a retrospective examination and cannot be undertaken at the time events take place. The retrospective element in oral history is important because it asks questions of the past which reflect present interests and seeks evidence which was not produced at the time. That evidence is collected within a changed culture and, therefore, is not vulnerable to the biases and pressures of the period which produced it however much it may be shaped by the biases of its own day. For example, the Berkeley campus has such a contemporary oral history programme and we are informed that it is one:

> . . . where the alumni as fundors directly control the choice of informants for the university history programme. As a result, not merely have all the student leaders who convulsed the university during the 1960s been ignored, but President Clark Kerr himself has been banned.[4]

One often needs a period of perhaps a decade or more – when participants are in retirement or otherwise beyond the power structure of organizations – before they are in a position to speak openly about particular organizations or events. But this reminds us that institutions continue and unless the funding body is attempting to fund objective research then the chances of an open record are not good. It is another reminder that contiguity does not guarantee 'truth'; indeed, contemporary investigation may well prove less compatible with truth than retrospection.

In sum and in brief, my definition of oral evidence is *an account of first hand experience recalled retrospectively, communicated to an interviewer for historical purposes and preserved on a system of reproducible sound*. And here I have self-consciously changed my terminology from oral 'history' to oral 'evidence'. In practice few make the distinction between oral history as the raw 'personal testimony' collected by such an interview and the written 'historical account' using it as evidence. This could be the analysis of a single interview but will usually include many interviews and the usual range of historical sources. I do not maintain the distinction in the text because the collection of oral testimony can proceed successfully whether it is called 'evidence' or 'history'. But the process of using interviews to move from the biography of the individual to the social dimension of an historical account is, for me, also part of the definition and practice of oral 'history'.

Part Two   Creating the Interviews

4   The informants

As Anthony Mason puts it: 'if you want to talk to the people who knew
Lloyd George in 1916, you can probably contact all those now living.
The social historian . . . who wants to discover the nature and structure of working class family life before 1914 has to sample, and this is
an area of social science shot through with difficulty.'

Brian Harrison
'Oral History and Recent Political History', *Oral History*, **1**, no. 3,
p. 40

Sampling is a highly developed procedure in the social sciences; but
just as an awareness of social science methodology can enhance the
practice of oral history, too much attention to it would be unduly
inhibiting. It would be the worst kind of foolishness not to interview
informative centenarians simply because their background excluded them from one's sample. On the other hand, the value of any
one such interview is greatly enhanced if it can be placed into
comparative context with others. In practice researchers who want
their work to be representative of collective experience conduct
interviews with informants from the same location, occupation,
factory, religious organization, sports club or whatever is the subject of interest. It is then assumed that the experiences of those
interviewed will give a representative picture of that experience in
general. In methodological terms one is generalizing from a sample
of the population. Sampling has always been used as a practical
procedure. Merchants took only a sample of their grain to the Corn
Exchange, shop customers taste only one grape to know the flavour
and so forth. It is assumed that the one will represent all – and so it
will if it is a fairly drawn sample not chosen from only the largest
grains of wheat or the ripest bunch of grapes.

Clearly the degree to which an oral history needs to concern itself
with sampling will depend on the nature of the project. If the subject
is a social history then it is essential to attempt to collect all types of
experience or to be aware of the experience which has not been

recorded; if the subject is a famous person then sampling is irrelevant and one simply interviews those who knew the person. But even in this latter case the final account will be distorted if only respectable contacts from their public and family life are interviewed and not their dissolute companions – assuming they had some – or if the sample of informants were drawn only from supporters not opponents. In other words the crucial point is always to ensure that the people we have interviewed provide (collectively) a representative picture. Because the experience we wish to sample is in the past and the whole population is no longer alive to be selected, oral historians cannot use statistically valid sampling: our use of sampling techniques can only *guide* our efforts to include all types of experience. Part of the usefulness comes from categorizing and classifying the interviews by such criteria after they have been collected. To do this effectively we need not only to be aware of the individual as representative of a type of social experience, but also to construct an interview schedule which will elicit that information, and to conduct interviews with a flexibility which will enable us to make the maximum historical use of them. We owe that much care and effort to those who willingly give their time and memories to the historical record.

Briefly and technically put, 'The theory and methods of sampling are based upon two concepts – that of the normal distributions, and that of independant random sampling – and upon theorems derived from these two concepts.'[1] The most widely known application of these procedures is by political pollsters. Although they interview comparatively few people they are able to generalize their findings from the opinions of a given number of individuals to claim that they represent the views of a particular constituency or even of the country. The data of the pollsters can also be broken down by a number of variables such as class, age, sex, trade union membership, house ownership, or, in principle, any social characteristic which has been systematically collected from each informant.

The classic and simplest sampling technique uses the 'random' sample where, for example, one might investigate some aspect of the lives of skilled workers by selecting for interview every 1000th skilled worker in the census returns, which would give a hundred interviews for every million so classified. In fact, random samples are rarely used as they are expensive to conduct, requiring a network of interviewers in every part of the country, which is costly in time and travel. A more frequently used technique is that of 'multistage' sampling which divides the 'population' into a number of areas with similar characteristics. Relevant characteristics for our example might be areas representing heavy and light industry, various types of skills, and areas of prosperity and decline; the country is thus divided into representative areas from which a number are randomly selected. The requisite number of individuals to be interviewed are then selected from within those few areas.

As one of the basic requirements of sampling theory is that everyone in the designated group should have an equal chance of being selected, no collection of oral history interviews is likely to be a random sample by social science standards. The contingencies of death, emigration and untraceability of the entire historic population would ensure that not all of the participants stood an equal chance of being selected for interview. This is an important issue for historical analysis. Oral historians can interview only survivors and we do not know how social and occupational factors may bias the typicality of the survivors. For example, I interviewed a number of East Anglian fishermen and discovered (according to my sample) that the majority drank very moderately, and this factor has affected my historical account of what was typical of their social and domestic life.[2] But when I commented on this to one fisherman he claimed to remember lots of hard-drinking fishermen and added the observation that 'drunkards die young', with the implication that most of the heavy drinkers had not survived long enough for me to interview. Now whether or not his intuitive wisdom is correct in this particular case, it is a good example of how the historical and social experience of one's interviewees might have affected the type of person who survived to be interviewed, and how that could affect an historical account based on that evidence. In that example one cannot estimate how representative my sample was in that respect because one does not know either what proportion of fishermen drank heavily or how any such drinking has affected their proportionate survival. But clearly if the 'sample' of fishermen is biased to those with the healthiest lifestyles then any account based on their experiences is going to relect that bias. It is, incidentally, also an excellent example of how one's informants contribute to the interpretation of the information as well as providing it.

Domestic service can be used to demonstrate the utility of sampling even within a single occupation. A history of domestic work based on interviews taken mainly from servants who worked in grand houses employing a dozen or so servants would give an image of working life far removed from the reality of most servants. As *individual* accounts of life in the servants' hall, the servant hierarchy, the servants' Christmas ball, the move from town to country with the social calendar, and so on, they may well be absolutely authentic; but they would be the experiences of only a minority of servants. Most domestic servants were employed in middle-class homes which employed only one or two servants. The majority of servants led isolated and lonely lives and to allow the experience of the minority to stand as *typical* of domestic service would be most false. It would be bad history. Interviewing even a large number of servants would not necessarily give one a basis for a sound generalization as to the occupational experience of servants. Even if one altered the focus of the study from 'domestic servants' to 'domestic servants in large households' one could still get a distorted picture if one interviewed only senior servants such as butlers and housekeepers; their views on the satisfactions of being a servant would inevitably be coloured by the degree of their own success; to get an accurate impression one would also need to interview those who remained lower servants throughout their career. It would also be revealing to interview those who tried the occupation and left it because they would not tolerate the conditions of employment.

Similar biases could occur if the impression of a particular industry was based on a number of interviews with informants who had worked all their lives in an industry where short-term casual employment was the normal work-pattern. By definition, where long service was rare, those workers who did stay are liable to have attitudes to the work and their employers different from those who did not stay long. Yet it is often just such workers who become informants simply because even in retirement they are known by their particular occupation and researchers are directed towards them: those who worked only a brief time in an occupation are known by their subsequent employments and rarely traced. Similar factors which might make particular interviewees atypical of their group would include the breadwinner being in continuous employment in an occupation where casual work and short-time were usual, or a family having only one child where large families were normal. Either factor would make that life experience materially superior to the majority of that historical group. This is not to say that such accounts are not interesting and informative but simply that they should not be taken as representative of more than a minority. These pitfalls would be obvious were informants to be traced through a firm's occupational pension scheme, or selected from a trade union retirement home. It would create a false impression of the workers' attitude to their employer in the first case and the level of union activity in the other if general impressions of the industry were drawn from such sources. On the other hand if one specifically wants to sample the experience of deferential or of militant workers then they are liable to prove ideal locations to find such informants.

The above are rather obvious examples of the grosser distortions which can enter into an analysis of information based on an ill-considered collection of interviews, however valuable and interesting each interview may be in its own right. And although oral history cannot make use of sampling with any technical rigour, 'quota' sampling provides a framework within which the degree of representativeness can be analysed. This method requires only that the general size and distribution of the group to be investigated are already known. Paul Thompson was the first to apply this method in establishing the Oral History Archive at Essex University. Started in 1968 the project took a quota sample of 444 informants selected to represent the population of England, Wales and Scotland. The sample was drawn from the 1911 occupational census and was designed to give a proportionate sample of the work and family experience from informants across the whole range of classes from unskilled to professional. The selection was further controlled by ensuring that it contained the correct proportion of men and women and that these reflected regional populations as well as rural, urban and city dwellers. Now while this was not a random sample in that one could not sample the actual population of 1911, interviewers had to find and record those who had survived from that period. This means that the interviews are not simply a haphazard number of individual accounts but are broadly representative of the social experience of a period. They provide the potential for general conclusions about the comparative standard of living between classes, within classes, between regions and so forth.[3]

My research on the fishing industry of East Anglia was directed by Paul Thompson as an addition to the archive, and it applied the same principles to a single industry and region. This ensured that the people selected for interview reflected the various types of experience within the fishing industry. The project allowed for sixty interviews with fishermen or the women from fishing families. Had I simply gone and interviewed the first sixty 'fishermen' I found there is little doubt that, as *individual* accounts, they would have been as informative as those which were collected. But, given the variety of experience to be found in even one occupation in a single region, they would have been most unlikely to have included the full range of experience. Finding informants with quota sampling in mind obliged me to seek an appropriate number of informants who worked in the steam drifting, sail trawling and the inshore sectors. I also had to find those who worked in the various crew positions, not just skippers whose status in the community meant that they were almost invariably suggested to me as the most suitable informants. As the industry contained a number of fishermen-owners I needed to interview the self-employed as well as the employers and employees. A balanced view of industrial relations and working conditions could emerge only through interviewing all sections. But occupation is not the only area of experience which affects attitudes and values: many of these are formed before starting work and so it was important to include the different localities and communities the fishermen had lived in, such as rural and urban areas. Subsequent analysis of the interviews confirmed how constructive this sampling had been, because there were marked differences in social attitudes between the coastal villages where fishermen predominated and the rural villages where the fishermen were in a minority. The resulting collection of interviews is much more informative because, instead of simply being able to analyse the result as the experience of 'fishermen', it is possible to compare and contrast the values and attitudes of the various sectors within the industry and from various locations within the region. In other words, instead of being simply a collection of individual biographical reminiscences it is now sociologically and historically more informative. In this case the utility is further increased because this project used fundamentally the same interview schedule that Paul Thompson and Thea Vigne evolved for the original project in the Essex Oral History Archive (I changed the section on work to suit the occupation) and so the material can be integrated with that project to provide a larger sample in the appropriate categories.

If oral interviews are to be used as a systematic source from which to make general historical statements we must be aware of what sort of experience our interviews represent – and which areas of experience they leave untapped. A piece of research from Canada illustrates this point. Jane Synge interviewed people born between 1890 and 1908, using a quota sample of various socio-economic groups from both industry and agriculture focusing on '. . . how families coped with such crises and potential crises as care of the aged, bereavement, orphanhood and unemployment.'[4] This quota approach should have provided the basis for a sound analytical study, the results of which could be taken as typical of the population at large. But as she writes:

> Analysis of the experience of successive cohorts shows the extent to which the family lives described by my respondents were atypical of those of the whole adult population of the early twentieth century. . . . Our respondents are talking of homes with children. But of the cohort born in 1890, who reached adulthood, 41 percent either did not marry or were childless.[5]

This emphasizes the point that oral historians are interviewing only survivors and had Synge not been alert to the limitations of her material the experience of little more than half the population would have been accepted as the experience of all. She acknowledges that:

> . . . had I examined the demographic patterns of the era more closely prior to the development of the questionnaire, I would have recognized the importance of studying the high incidence of bachelorhood, spinsterhood and childlessness and would have introduced specific questions to elicit more detailed material on the lives of unmarried and/or childless relatives and neighbours.[6]

As it stands she did collect quite a lot of evidence about the unmarried and childless simply because her informants talked about the unmarried and childless relatives who lived with them or the nature of their family's contact with other kin. This is one of the great strengths of oral history; one is not collecting only biographical material, but the informants' observations of their wider social world: they can tell you something of how other people behaved. And if the opportunity to use this material in a systematic, rather than anecdotal, manner has been lost in this case because this aspect of representativeness was not foreseen, it is unlikely to have even been identified had Synge not been alert to the significance of sampling.

In order to be able to place informants into different quota categories it is necessary to collect the relevant information from each one. Because of this it is as well to consider some information as being virtually an essential part of any oral history interview. It is only by being able to place a person into the context of their class, location and time that the full potential of the account can be utilized. If a wide spectrum of information which permits classification is collected it also allows the quota categories to be constructed and reconstructed according to the research interests of the different users of an archive. Such flexibility and potential can be realized only if systematic thought is given to the content of an interview schedule and the interviewers implement it with as much rigour as is compatible with good open-ended interviewing.

5   The interview schedule

People using the tape recorder, like those using the computer, discover quickly however, that it does not have intrinsic magic. Without the historical and sociological imagination shaping the interview, one can end up recording miles of meaningless information.

Tamara, K. Haraven
'The Search for Generational Memory: Tribal Rites in Industrial Society', *Daedalus*, no. 4, 1978, p. 141

There is a vast literature on the subject of questionnaire design: most oral historians will be none the worse for not having read it.[1] Nevertheless, survey methodology's central concerns have been to develop techniques which will guarantee a straight answer to a straight question as well as the technical and statistical methods of interpreting such answers. As surveys are well-established and widely used their method of constructing a verifiable system for collecting information cannot be ignored. Indeed it is used as a proven standard from which to criticize the methodology of oral history, or rather the lack of it, as most oral historians do not discuss their methodology but appear to work on the common-sense assumption that in a face to face interview one obtains a more or less useful account of the past. It will be useful, therefore, to start by considering, very briefly, the concerns of survey questionnaires before moving on to what they might teach us about asking questions in oral history. After all oral historians want answers to questions and if they do not believe that these are most successfully obtained through questionnaires they should at least argue the grounds of their objections.

Survey techniques are based on the theories and concepts of positivistic social science and mathematics. The essence of their activity is to collect a limited range of information from a large number of people. The largest application of this type of work is the decennial census which sets out to survey the entire population. The census is basically concerned with counting heads, but it also collects information on occupations, ages, gender and other information of a factual kind. Survey methods are widely employed by governments as well as commercial organizations, political parties and anyone else who wants to collect information at a predictable and economical cost. Informants are not perceived as individuals who may be more or less informative and who might be capable of giving a wider perspective on the subject of inquiry. The scope of inquiry has been defined in advance, that is to say the variables which are to be collected for analysis have been decided upon in the light of existing concepts and theories.[2] The answers to questions are treated as individual 'facts' which can then be aggregated and correlated with other similar individual facts. Surveys often have a very specific purpose and want to spend the minimum time discovering which of two or three candidates will win an election, why people choose brand X, whether sections of the business world are expecting to expand or contract in the next quarter, whether a consumer article is chosen for its style, durability or price and so on. These aspects may then be divided by special groups. For example, manufacturers may want to know in detail who their customers actually are, whether they are mainly the 20–29 or the 50–59 age group, mainly men or women, skilled working or lower middle-class, and so on; this information can then be used to influence the type of advertising and where it is placed and similar marketing decisions. In other words they want information about people's attitudes and activities and they want to know how representative it is of the population at large. This is just what a historian might like to know about the distribution of politics, leisure, religion or some other activity in the past. But whereas oral history interviews will tape hours of conversation which will be analysed at a later stage, survey techniques are limited in the amount of contact that they allow with informants, partly because of the cost to whoever commissioned the project, and partly because few people are willing to give much of their time to that sort of enterprise.

Survey questionnaire design and use, therefore, has very different assumptions and conditions from those of oral history. They require answers which can be numerically processed with the minimum of preparation and so usually limit the choice of answers to pre-planned categories. Quite often informants are asked to respond to a proposition in terms of a five point scale from 'Strongly agree', 'Agree' through 'Neutral' to 'Disagree' and 'Strongly disagree': all the interviewer needs to do is to enter a number from 1 to

5 in the appropriate box and the information is ready to be fed into a computer. The questionnaires are completed by a staff of interviewers whose expertise lies not in the subject of the inquiry but in the art of asking questions as instructed and field-coding the answers. The survey designers assume that provided the stimuli are the same, the same questions are asked in the same order in the same neutral tone, then differences in the answers can be assumed to be due to the different opinion or circumstance of the informant (other factors biasing responses such as the gender, age, class or race of the informant/interviewer will be discussed in the following chapter). All the emphasis is on the pre-planning and testing of questions so that the actual interviewing is seen as a mere mechanical completion of a task.

Survey questionnaires are concerned with the technique of formulating questions so that they mean the same thing to everyone. For example, one might ask 'Are class divisions important?' and no doubt most people would provide a response which could be coded in terms of a five point scale. What, however, would be the significance of an answer coded (4) 'Unimportant' in terms of meaning? It could be that the informants responded to the question in terms of their personal attitude and are signifying that they are neither snobbish nor deferential in their attitude to people from different classes; it is unimportant in their evaluation of individuals. The same person, however, could also believe that class is 'very important' as a social factor in affecting the general quality of life, economic performance, or industrial attitudes. Naturally no survey would be so naive as to ask such a poorly formulated question as the object in devising closed questions is to refine the precision of a question so that the response has to address itself to the specific area intended by the researcher. The degree to which a question achieves consistency in being understood by all informants in the same sense is referred to as a question's 'reliability'. The method cannot, therefore, allow interviewers to rephrase questions because they would then be collecting responses to lots of different questions rather than the planned number of responses to the same questions.

Another methodological issue relevant to oral historians is the 'validity' of an answer. Validity refers to the degree to which a question elicits responses which actually serve as an indicator of what it intends to measure. For example, it might be assumed that a series of questions about occupation, wages and salaries would indicate a person's 'income'. But this would not be so unless the questions revealed any alternative sources of finance from capital or occasional employment. If a question on 'earnings' elicited answers which simply cited the basic wage without including bonuses or overtime then it would be an 'unreliable' question and would need rephrasing or supplementary questions.

In sum the survey type interview is geared to gathering information through a series of elementary questions which allow only limited responses and which are codable for numerical processing. If the method has developed a high level of methodological sophistication and can collect worthwhile data on certain areas it also has its disadvantages. Because of the need to collect and process the data at economic cost the methodological tail wags the substantive dog. The method dictates a limited range of responses and does not explore their meaning for the individual, assuming that the method will ensure that the questions have a shared meaning for all.

What happens in oral history is very different. The interview must allow informants to provide understandable accounts of social and historical experience, which are valid and reliable in the broadest sense, so that another interviewer would not gain a substantially different account of that experience. For if the information changes substance from interview to interview then oral evidence is not a reliable source. The way in which an interview schedule might improve the value of the evidence should be considered by all those who undertake interviews. It is not simply a question of gaining authentic information but also of utilizing it. It is of little value to the study of history if oral evidence simply piles up in archives in an indigestible mass because lack of thought and method has made it impossible to use systematically and constructively.

From the expansion of oral history in the early 1970s a number of oral historians have rather objected to the use of prepared questions. As one of the motives behind oral history was to collect the experience of those under-represented in the historical record, it was felt that informants should be allowed to relate their experience in terms of their own priorities and interests and not through the interests of the largely middle-class academics who were interviewing them. Letting people speak for themselves and showing a welcome deference to the experience of others was felt to be achieved best by simply letting informants relate what interested them in their own way with only a minimum intervention from the interviewer. The ideal was a completely unstructured interview where

conversation followed the direction given by the informant. This
may or may not occasionally get good results. But the content of
each interview will be different according to the main interests of
the informant. That would be fine if the aim of oral history was to
collect lots of biographies: but I take its aim to be the collection of
historical evidence and this means that researchers should not duck
their responsibility for deciding how evidence should be collected in
the most historically useful manner. Informants may know what is
important to their lives (although it is unsafe to assume that they will
tell it without prompting) but that is not the same as knowing what is
important for the historical record. Some informants start their
account by groping for memories of coronations, royal deaths,
visiting dignitaries and civic events of various kinds, in a word
'history' as they were taught it in the classroom. It often requires a
series of questions on the minutiae of their direct experiences to
assure them that the interviewer really does want to know about
their (unremarkable) lives. Researchers should not aspire to a non-
interventionary role somehow assuming that this results in less biased
information. After all they are initiating the collection and if they do
not know what they are looking for, nor why, they might shelve the
attempt until they do. Naturally one will learn from the informants.
The first few interviews of any project are almost certain to show
that some of the lines of inquiry are ill-conceived and the information volunteered by the informants has shed new light on issues,
given new perspectives and suggested new lines of inquiry. Using a
schedule does not mean that the informants are treated as mere
providers of 'facts', but that where they make a valuable contribution it is systematically incorporated into the study and improves the
quality of other interviews. One precise advantage of oral evidence
is that it is interactive and one is not left alone, as with documentary
evidence, to divine its significance; the 'source' can reflect upon the
content and offer interpretation as well as facts.

Few oral historians today would advocate such an unstructured
approach and now much of the debate over oral history practice is
encapsulated in whether the questions one wants to ask are seen as
an interview 'schedule' or as an interview 'questionnaire'. A 'questionnaire' indicates a set of questions which are to be asked of each
informant in order to ensure that one has an answer to every
question, that is to say, a style rather close to the traditional social
survey approach. A 'schedule', on the other hand, is regarded as
little more than an aide-mémoire to ensure that the interviewer will

remember to prompt the informant on all those areas the research is to cover. My own view is that aspects of both approaches can be used to advantage – the questionnaire approach when planning the research, deciding what information is relevant and the areas of discussion which might throw light on these, and the schedule approach when actually interviewing; thus combining the strengths of both approaches.

The starting point for composing an oral history interview schedule is an exercise of the historical and sociological imagination. Here one cannot discuss specific content because the subjects for research are so varied and different in scope. Interviews can be used to record something as unique as the development of a specific scientific invention in which only a few people were involved and where, because the result is *known*, the focus is on the detailed process of discovery and development; on the other hand the object of the research may be to *discover* the economic, social, political and cultural life of an entire community. In the former one might be interested in only a few years or even months of a person's life, in the other their lifelong experience. Clearly the work which can be done through oral history in any particular region will be dependent on the history of the area and the experience of the people. Typical of specific research projects are those looking at the history of a certain craft, industry or company; or those which are defined more by geography focusing on a town, village or community.[3] Such variety precludes any specific advice. Nevertheless, where interviews are being conducted with the aim of establishing an archive of general historical information through oral evidence there are some general points worth making. The remarks which follow are written with the latter approach in mind, that is to say a project where the main aim is to collect a wide range of experience which can then be used to shed light on a variety of questions social historians might pose about the period.

The main issue must be to consider how a schedule improves the collection, authenticity and use of oral evidence. Take collecting first. The great advantage of an interview questionnaire is that it constrains us to reflect upon just what we are trying to add to the historical record and how the experience of the informant might enhance that knowledge. It also constrains us to consider how a number of interviews together might be used to construct a general picture of a particular period, community or occupation. That is best achieved by ensuring that every informant is asked to relate the same areas of experience in order that comparisons between different periods, places and groups can be made. This process of planning questions is not solely a methodological issue, it is also fundamental to formulating the conceptual issues. For example, assume that one wanted to discover whether a particular local craft or skill regarded itself as an elite stratum within the working class, or even as lower middle class. In order to be able to contribute to the debate on class structures and formations, one has to decide which areas of experience and questions would actually reveal class position, activity, attitudes and values. Just going along to have them talk about their 'lives' or the 'old days' will undoubtedly result in a good deal of fascinating reminiscence, but with each informant giving details on different aspects of their experience and saying little or nothing about others the opportunity of systematic use would be greatly diminished. One needs to start by asking oneself what it is that one is trying to discover – if it is worth asking one informant their experience in that area it is worth asking another. All the informants will add what they consider of interest to the interview; our task is to be clear what we would like to know – if it is worth asking one informant in a particular location it is worth asking another.

It is not sufficient, however, simply to collect systematically information which is valid and reliable in terms of what is related and recorded. Part of the authenticity of survey research comes from its known cultural context: it is contemporary. In time this information will become part of the historical record of a given date. Oral history evidence does not automatically possess this essential and known time provenance because an interview usually ranges across various time periods. It also lacks a known provenance in social and geographical location unless the informants are questioned in detail about their background and movements as well as the time of whatever event is recounted. For example, an account (or document for that matter) of weekly wages or prices of various commodities is not very useful unless it can be dated; earnings and prices which were unremarkable in one period are exceptional in another. Unless the information can be located in time it adds little to our historical knowledge. The same is true of working conditions or social customs; unless the account can be placed into a social context it contributes little to historical explanation. And yet, I have listened to interviews which gave a very full and interesting account of working life in which the interviewer had not asked even one question as to the period; presumably because both the informant and the interviewer knew, neither actually made this shared knowledge overt by ensuring that it was included on the tape. Any interview should ensure that information has the maximum provenance possible and the best way of ensuring that is to have thought about the questions which will elicit it.

Time is the most obvious required provenance for any historical information and must be established in all interviews; it is an essential requirement for any questionnaire. In Chapter 7 (p. 77) there is an example of how, by a slip of the tongue, an informant can place an incident in the wrong period. Although fairly obvious in that case, such errors can be difficult to resolve unless picked up at the time of the interview: they can always make the search for confirmatory material much more time consuming.

Of equal importance is *location*, both social and geographical. A person's class position is essential to the understanding of their social and cultural experience. Eventually a person's class location will largely depend on their own occupational history and the degree of social mobility which they undergo. But oral history is very valuable in being able to use memories of childhood as historical evidence for the patterns of economic, cultural and domestic life in their social and economic location. As childhood situation depends on the parents' occupations only very limited use can be made of childhood memories unless the parents' social location is clearly established. The occupation and social backgrounds of the father and mother *must* be asked if the information about the informant's early years is to be placed in a proper context. Questions about mother and father are essential, questions about the grandparents desirable. Domestic comfort and even values and attitudes are often directly influenced by the amount of support given by relatives, most usually the grandparents, so going back to the third generation for basic information about the grandparents' occupations is a valuable context within which to place the experience of the informant. Indeed, the occupations and amount of contact with any family members is worth including. Similarly where an informant is married, the occupation and background of their spouse is also relevant. Studies of social mobility have traditionally taken the male occupation as the main determinant, but oral history provides the opportunity to collect information on a number of factors affecting a person's subsequent career. I would suspect, for example, that an analysis of a number of interviews might show that at the level of the skilled working class the move to white collar occupations could be due to the educational level and social background of the mother rather than the occupation of the father. Clearly the more one knows about the social context of the family, rather than merely the individual, the more understandable the life of the individual becomes. But not every informant can be expected, when approached to talk about their own life, to spontaneously mention all these aspects without prompting, nor any interviewer to prompt for them without having prepared the questions in advance.

The value of consistency in covering topics is illustrated by my own work on fishermen, where I asked them all about the role superstition played in their work. If I had merely left it to be mentioned by those to whom it was an important or memorable part of their life (and who thought that it was an interesting enough historical subject to volunteer to me) I would have undoubtedly collected enough accounts to have indicated that superstition was important to some fishermen. Because the question was asked of everyone the pattern of its location and use according to the type of fishing became apparent. Had it been collected as information volunteered only by some informants it would have appeared as simple individual quirks of credulity instead of socially shaped by the industrial location – being more prevalant in some types of fishing than in others and more firmly held by authority figures. When I started the interviews it was a subject which did not interest me and I included it in the questionnaire only because all the secondary literature on the subject indicated that it was an important part of the fishermen's consciousness and practice. So having the questions on superstition pre-planned and ready to use at appropriate points in the conversation was also an essential discipline to ensure that I elicited the information. As it happened the questions gave valuable insights to their views on luck, which were in turn related to their attitude to the market price of fish and through that to the level of their earnings and their industrial attitudes. I would not have collected that information consistently enough had I left it to the informant to guide the interview, or to my own interest, and it could be that the most valuable function of a questionnaire is to compel interviewers to do better than they might without one.

Having planned questions and thought about possible answers one should become more sensitized to the status of the information being collected. It is possible to collect a long and fascinating account of local religious divisions, rivalries and so forth, perhaps describing all the denominations in the neighbourhood, but on reviewing the interview or trying to categorize the informant's religion discover that this was never actually expressed. It would have taken only one prepared question to have elicited this information and to fail to do so is to miss the chance to relate religious views to other areas of experience and attitudes: it must surely also make it more difficult to assess any likely bias in the account of the relationship between the various denominations. In any interview informants will make generally descriptive statements such as 'Not many people used to go to the church', the meaning of which appears obvious. But one needs to have thought about what answers are required to understand the experience. Is such an answer based on the fact that the informants were of those few who went to church and reply from their own observations of the size of the congregations? Or is it based only on the observation that few of their neighbours or friends attended a place of worship? The information is historically useful in both cases, but needs rather different evaluation according to the circumstances of the informants. Similarly if religion is a historical dimension worth inquiring into then it is only sensible to have prepared questions to elicit how often and for what occasions the informant(s) attended a place of worship. Close involvement with religion might throw light on their leisure habits, industrial attitudes and so forth, and if anyone ever wishes to use the interviews to investigate the effect of religious affiliations on other dimensions of experience then, unless that sort of information has been collected from all, it is not possible. Similarly in talking about politics one might hope to record the politics of the informant's parents and even kin or workmates so as to provide some glimpse of the political traditions and culture within which their individual politics were shaped. In other words the evidence gains maximum utility by ensuring a mixture of personal experience and attitudes plus social observation and comment: the nature of personal experience can only be fully appreciated within the context of the social.

My own preference is for questions of detail. I believe, for example, that when talking about childhood experience it is an advantage to ask detailed questions about what furniture, floor covering, pictures, ornaments and so forth were in the room, as recalling material details helps the informant more readily to recapture the thought and feelings of the period. Also such detail can be used by different researchers in various ways; it can be used to establish material differences between strata, the cultural activities within the home through knowledge of books, music and activities, the use of space and so on. Factual recall of the daily round and routine is perhaps the most useful approach to interviewing for an archive because it does allow a variety of uses and interpretations. Nevertheless, it can be useful to ask about alternatives to actual experience. Asking informants whether they ever considered entering into a different job when they left school, for example, might reveal that one of their parents would not let them enter the occupation of their choice – as where a mother will not let a daughter enter domestic service because of her own experience of it, or factory work because it was considered low status. An exploration of some of the more likely possible alternatives can be useful indicators of values, aspirations and status boundaries.

Where the research is a group project probably the best means of ensuring that everyone understands and shares the objectives of the research is to design a questionnaire collectively. Laying out questions in detail is also advantageous where research is to be carried out over a wide area employing local interviewers. A list of detailed questions demonstrates the sort of information one is hoping the informant would relate during the course of an unprompted interview were it an ideal world. It also enables the person who enjoys interviewing, but who has little historical knowledge, to collect more useful information than he or she would otherwise have done. Such a procedure is also essential where there is a continuing programme of research; for instance where firms interview retiring personnel (usually limited to executive and managerial grades) for the business history of the firm. A useful addendum to the questionnaire is a brief statement laying out the intentions of the research and purpose of the questions included, as this enables the interviewer to work creatively and change the wording to suit the occasion while still probing in the right directions. A good questionnaire, with appropriate notes, will probably prove the most useful reference document that users of the material who have not been involved in its collection could have, short of a fully indexed or computerized archive.

The danger of the general life history questionnaire approach lies in having too many areas of experience on which one would like some information. It is possible, especially where time and funding do not allow for sufficient time to interview at the required length, that the interview will gradually move from being an open-ended exploration of the informant's experiences and world view and degenerate into a series of questions and answers which need to be completed. This should be avoided at all costs for inept interviewing will largely nullify the advantages of good preparation.

If an interview schedule appears to be inhibitory it need not be used. But the advantage of all the thought which has gone into its preparation will remain in the interviewers' minds and enable them to achieve far better results than if no schedule had been prepared. Many people consider history to be about the rich and powerful and are too modest to volunteer information at length: the interviewers have a duty to accept responsibility for preparing themselves with enough informed curiosity to stimulate the informants to feel it is worth conveying their experience. Far from a schedule inhibiting interviewees, as some believe, it has been my experience that potential informants have agreed to be interviewed on seeing an interview schedule and being convinced that I had 'hundreds' of questions to ask them: their reluctance was partly due to a fear of being placed in an uncomfortable social situation, whereby a stranger visits them to talk about their life and they really do not know what to talk about and feel that they have nothing of interest to volunteer. Once assured that the interviewer is interested and is prepared to seek information rather than expect them to take the initiative in volunteering it, most people are more than willing to be interviewed.

6   The interview

> . . . we can now go into an interview with all the assurance that we are working to bring about a new departure. Each of us according to the light he has is helping to bring back *man* into history – not man mediated through trends, movements, distribution maps and statistics, but man himself, men and women in the flesh. And it is this direct contact which I believe works through a kind of osmosis, through your skin so to speak, to give the feel of history, a sense of the past which is such an essential ingredient to the best historical writing.
>
> George Ewart Evans
> 'Approaches to Interviewing', *Oral History*, **1,** no. 4, 1973, p. 71

Interviewing is fundamentally a process of asking people about a set of circumstances which they have experienced. This simple process has been the subject of a seemingly endless methodological scrutiny much of which is concerned with the interview as practised in social surveys. This is not an appropriate model for oral historians. Oral history interviewing is more constructively located within the ethnomethodological approach to collecting social knowledge with its emphasis on interpersonal dynamics. This accepts that individuals present a different image of themselves to different people and at different times so that no single account of themselves will ever be complete or quite the same as an account given on a different occasion. There could hardly be two more varied approaches to obtaining authentic information. In the one the entire emphasis is on the inflexible, uniform and neutral behaviour of the interviewer with the informant responding simply to the form, content and sequence of the questions; which in themselves are formulated so as to limit the shape and extent of the answers. The other is of the informant and the interviewer being aware of each other as people and of setting about a common task of recording the experiences of the one in an open and conversational manner. Nevertheless, both are agreed that the situation is not value-free and that what is said will be different according to how the two people perceive and react to each other. Inevitably we perceive others as being of a given age, gender, social and ethnic group. These factors are generally obvious on first meeting and they have an initial effect on the way in which the informant and interviewer react to each other.

Gender cannot be a neutral social factor. There are conventions which affect the relationships between men and women, particularly between strangers where role expectations are the strongest. Any research into the history of childbirth would find that women were less willing to describe their experiences to a man than to a woman. A woman interviewer would be less likely to collect accounts from a man of bawdy nights out and drinking with pals than would a male interviewer. Those are obvious examples, but other less obviously sensitive areas will be affected by cross-gender interviewing as men and women present themselves differently to members of their own or the opposite sex. Women could be less willing to report holding non-traditional attitudes to their domestic and womanly role to a man than to a woman. This effect might be intensified if the female interviewer was also a feminist and encouraged those sort of responses (although as the overt ideology of the interviewer is also a factor biasing results being a feminist would mitigate the effect of being a male). Studies of cross-ethnic interviewing have shown than black informants are less willing to relate their experience of prejudice and harassment to white interviewers than to black. In a class conscious society such as Britain informants perceive interviewers as of their class or of the one above or below them. This can affect what they say in front of that person, how they say it and, even more crucially, what they feel it inappropriate to say. Not surprisingly the ages of interviewers/interviewees has a strong effect on responses, with the most status exaggeration coming from those interviews between two people of similar age and opposite sex. Informants present themselves in the most status enhancing way because, on the whole, they want to impress people of their own age but of the opposite sex.

Most of the studies which reveal these biases have been carried out by those trying to improve the quality of survey research methods. They are, therefore, measuring the effect of the above factors on interviews which are brief, using closed questions and field-coding. These studies have also shown that other substantial sources of error come from the interviewers' biases in interpreting the informants' answers when coding them; indeed, as they are usually paid by results many interviewers invent responses in order to be remunerated for incomplete interviews. The basic difficulty in getting significant information from this approach stems from assumptions about the value of 'objectivity' conceived as a sterile space where both interviewer and interviewee are supposed to ask and answer questions in a social and contextual vacuum for purposes in which neither may have any genuine interest. But interviewers who are instructed to be non-committal and unbiased cannot avoid the interviewee perceiving them as an individual and their attempts to be non-committal may be seen as lack of interest, disapproval or even hostility. Informants have a very different perception of objectivity from the designers of survey research and one will gain a more accurate account by demonstrating a positive empathy for the point of view and life of the informant than by remaining aloof and unresponsive.

Much of this need not worry the oral historian unduly because many of the experiments designed to discover bias and defects in survey interviewing depend on recording them. Our procedure obviously eliminates errors of faulty recall, coding and note-taking (which is why one insists that oral history should be recorded). As the typical oral history interview is between people of different ages it is less subject to age bias, and because it is about the past status differences are less important than in the case of contemporary social surveys. Even more positively the circumstance and content of oral history interviews are such as to maximize authenticity because they revolve around the informants and involve them to the maximum possible:

> . . . validity may be conceived as increasing with *task* involvement; to the extent that a respondent's reaction derives from social or interpersonal involvement, we may expect it to result in bias, since, under such conditions, the response will be primarily a function of the relation between the respondent and the interviewer, instead of a response to the task.[1]

The importance of making the interview a task orientated activity is the essence of a good interview and we will return to that in a moment. First let us consider the importance of the rest of the remark to the effect that bias will result from the degree of social or interpersonal involvement and just what that means. As a hypothetical example imagine an interview by, or on behalf of, the management of a firm which was inquiring into the amount of informal working practices, including fiddling expense sheets, taking material, claiming unworked overtime and so forth. Certainly one would expect a very high degree of bias in that it would be unreasonable to assume that those involved would tell the truth and so risk the sack, even criminal prosecution, or, at the very least, an end to some pleasant perks once the firm had learned all about them. In other words although the degree of interpersonal involvement between the interviewer/interviewee is contemporary and important, the 'task' of recording the truth is not shared by both parties. What, however, if it were the case that a university department was investigating working practices from the point of view of pure academic research and neither the informants nor the firms would be identified? That should have greater success in getting at the truth, but one suspects that some people would doubt whether the information would remain unidentifiable and that if they spoke freely their own management might be able to identify them. A degree of deception and concealment could still be expected. What then of the oral historian asking about such practices at the workplace of fifty years ago, from workers long retired? The informants have no powerful reasons to conceal whatever was the genuine situation. They can neither be sacked nor penalized, they are not putting others at risk of those penalties, the information is, in that direct sense, of no contemporary power, it is historical. As so much social science interviewing is concerned with contemporary issues where the person's present situation and ego are directly involved, there are bound to be formidable difficulties in obtaining frank answers: once those difficulties are removed by discussing the *past* then the interview situation and the degree of bias and the means of overcoming it are radically transformed. In the above example a person might still conceal having been involved in 'fiddles' at work from a sense of wanting to present a respectable image, but certainly the motivation is nowhere near as strong as when it is a contemporary issue. Anyone who has practical experience of interviewing will know that people sometimes disassociate themselves from aspects of their past and that this can be encouraged by appropriate interviewing.

The distancing of time and place does help both participants in an interview to be open: life was different in the past, with different norms and standards. It is worth building on this natural advantage by forming questions in a way which suggests that some things which one might not be proud of in the present were common in the past and that you would expect the informant to have shared that experience. For example, it is now thought less appropriate to use heavy corporal punishment to control children, so if asked directly informants might be reluctant to acknowledge that their parents used such methods. They may feel that the interviewer would gain an impression of their parents by interpreting the answer in terms of today's values. But if the question is phrased to show that the interviewer accepts the values of the past as a normal assumption (for example, 'In those days many parents used a strap or cane to punish their children, what did your parents do?') it is easier for people to state the facts of heavy punishment without feeling that they are giving an impression of their parents which will be misconstrued. On the other hand, it will not oblige them to pretend to an experience they did not have. This type of question is known as 'sanctioning' from the fact that it allows someone to give an answer which they may have felt inhibited from giving if the interviewer had not paved the way. Some informants do this for themselves by prefacing an answer with 'Well, you must realize that things were different then . . .' or some similar remark when they feel that what they are about to say describes a situation so different from today's norms as to require justification. Consider this example, where I was beginning to ask an informant about his childhood home:

> *How many rooms were there in that house?*

> That one what I'm now referring to was by the name of Polky Lodge, and it's still standing. It was a double dweller, but now I believe it's all one house, and more or less modernised. It was up for sale a few weeks ago, a few months ago, for nine thousand pounds, which I suppose we could have bought it then for – nine pounds. But you see – there were no rules, regulations or restrictions about – a man with a wife and four children, he must have four rooms or anything of that sort. It was nothing of that type whatever. If a man had ten children and he went into a house with only one bedroom, that was nobody else's concern but his own, and his own wife. And it very often happened. That was the thing about it, and there was nothing you could do about it. You slept on the couch, you slept where you could. Or you slept in an armchair on some occasions.[2]

His response to that simple question starts with contemporary references, moves to stating that years ago the number of people in a house was a private matter and beyond control (creating his own 'sanctions' for their housing conditions) and, although he describes difficult sleeping arrangements, never answers the question. He was born in 1897 in Norfolk and was one of thirteen children most of whom were living at home during his childhood. From further descriptions it became clear that it was, at the most, a two-bedroomed cottage and may well have been one-bedroomed. Although asked a simple factual question he was immediately conscious of its implications with regard to a standard of 'respectability' which requires parents to sleep separately from children and brothers apart from sisters. Clearly one cannot prepare for all eventualities and sensitivities, but paving the way for an informant to speak openly and comfortably is the essence of good interviewing and it is something the interviewer should do for the informant where possible. In cases like this all one can do is agree with the informants and assure them that you are aware how much life has changed, and take the chance to reinforce the point that their recollections are important for those very reasons.

I have found that it is unusual for informants to be as sensitive on basic social conditions as the one cited above, and the following is a more typical response:

> [We had] . . . One room and a back room. The furniture was practically negligible. I remember all the beds – 'cos I was forced to sleep with my sisters. I used to – my three sisters slept at the top and I remember sleeping – more to our shame – I used to sleep at the bottom, crossways.[3]

Here the 'facts' of the situation are reported with a remark which acknowledges an awareness that their circumstances were less than ideal. But, it is in the past, and most informants feel sufficiently distanced from it to be able to report such conditions without discomfort. But the interviewer can self-consciously try to 'distance' topics which might be expected to cause difficulty. It is not easy to judge, particularly early in an interview, whether direct questions about sensitive topics will cause offence, so it is much easier to introduce the subject as a common assumption of other peoples' behaviour (for example, 'I believe many children had fleas in those days, was that true of children in your school?') and then follow up according to the answer (with, for example, 'Did you ever pick them up there?' or 'What did your mother do when you picked them up?'). In other words use the informants' knowledge about general social conditions to introduce and open up a topic, and then bring it to their direct experience of the subject. Indeed, where subjects are approached in this way the informants will often introduce their own level of experience without being asked a question. My experience leads me to believe that most informants are less defensive about their own experience in the past than is sometimes assumed, but there is no doubt that people do conceal those things they find embarrassing and any method of avoiding embarrassment will lead to a more authentic account.

Typically an interview might last for an hour or two and be repeated on another, or other, occasions. In the course of this the interviewer is usually treated as a guest and offered refreshments, or, at least, there are moments before and after the interview when conversation becomes more generally social and not confined to the past experience of the informant. During these periods the informant will often ask the interviewer questions about his or her background and origins. The interviewer cannot remain an anonymous questioner but must become known to the informant as a particular type of person. My own practice has been to make no comment on my own background unless my informant expresses curiosity. If interviewers start by ensuring (or insisting) that the informant knows about them there is the danger that the interviewer's background will be perceived as important and reacted to by the informant. The less strongly the interviewer's personal views and background are in evidence the less there will be to bias the informant. A sympathetic and interested listener is background enough if that is all the informant requires from the interviewer and the social situation.

A conscious exception to this practice of leaving it to the informant's curiosity to ask about the interviewer's background might be where the informant and the interviewer come from the same local community and know of each other. Many oral historians are interested in the history of their own locality, occupation or social institution so it is not uncommon for their background to be known to some of the people they interview. But a local farmer, or businessman, who decides to record the history of their own industry will have a particularly strong social identity as a local employer. This will make the initial stages of the interview more difficult because the ex-workers will be aware that any adverse comments about employers are actually a criticism of the person doing the interview. Similarly it can be difficult for someone who had been a domestic servant to be critical of the years of low pay, exploitation and social invisibility when interviewed by a local person known to come from the servant-keeping class. In these circumstances an informant can be inhibited from expressing experiences and opinions which have an implicit criticism of the interviewer's background and class. It runs counter to the canons of good behaviour to be overtly critical of a visitor and guest and as an interview *is* a social meeting this potential source of concealment and bias may best be faced openly. Where difficulties can be anticipated because of class (or other relevant dimension) it might be wise to acknowledge the difference in background by sanctioning it quite early in the interview by making an observation such as 'I think that you must have had a lot of complaints against your employer because my parents had servants and I know how low paid they were', so making it clear that you expect them to make critical observations. Distancing is also useful: 'Well it was years ago and the world has changed, neither of us would have the same opinions now' or a similar remark can make clear that you are not going to take the informant's views of employers 'then' as an implied criticism of yourself or even assume that it reflects their views of those employers 'now'. Such social differences are not necessarily a disadvantage and there are even some advantages in being far removed from the experience of the informant; as an 'outsider' one can ask for very detailed descriptions without artificiality. These differences can also be mitigated by emphasizing task commitment: convincing the informant that their honest responses are the only thing worth recording.

As everyone has a view of what constitutes normal and acceptable behaviour and values, some informants find difficulty in acknowledging aspects of their own life which they feel reflect badly on themselves or their family. Many informants would resist answering a direct negative to a question such as 'Did you have a good mother?'; the values associated with motherhood, family loyalty and social assumptions would prevent it. This is not to say that authentic and negative accounts of real situations cannot be obtained by interviewing. They will emerge if interviewing is both empathetic and meticulous; typically for example, informants who make generalized statements about what a good mother they had when the subject of relations with parents is raised, will, during the course of a detailed account of who did the housework, the shopping, how much leisure they had as a child, what treats and outings, then often begin to make more critical statements such as, 'I always thought my mother was hard on me making me do all that work'. But it is through questions of detail that these authentic memories and values can emerge, be expressed and recorded.

This approach of eliciting detailed factual recall has been criticized as too empirical by those who feel that it is more valuable to ask about values and attitudes to past events and relationships. One could agree with the aim without agreeing that it will be achieved through talking to an informant at the level of opinion and belief. It is those dimensions which are most likely to have been changed or clouded by time and changed circumstances. The accurate recall of any type of memory is more likely to be stimulated by immersing the informant in the detail of the past, and such detail does provide some check on the authenticity of expressed values. For example, little credence could be given to expressed values such as neighbourliness or a caring community if it is clear from the account of that person's life that in every hardship and crisis no one ever volunteered help when it was needed or, indeed, that they refused to help when asked. Consideration needs to have been given to which type of question will illuminate which area of experience (which includes values) and this is best done by advanced planning. The questions, however, are then flexibly applied in light of each particular informant. The crucial issue is that every question and probe should be fitted to the particular conversation and the logic of the social situation; their sequence cannot be planned in advance as survey methodology aims to do. Nevertheless, one must not fall into the opposite error of pretending that the interviewer does not exist and that the informants are simply telling their stories of their own accord. This seems to be the model imagined by some oral historians who feel that by identifying with the informants they somehow disappear as an 'interviewer' and simply let the informant talk. The issue of the intervention of the researcher is there and will not go away: we set up the interview for a purpose, and if we have no questions to ask, if we have no idea of what historical or theoretical issues the information is useful for – why on earth are *we* conducting interviews?

This reflects back to the importance of an interview schedule and the need to ask detailed questions. It is now a commonplace to state that informants will often volunteer a generalization which will prove inaccurate under detailed questioning. This can be due to a number of reasons: the informant is repeating a popularly held but erroneous view of the past, or is stating something which has come not from their own direct experience but from the media. The 'constraint of detail' is always needed to arrive at the genuine recall of the informant's own experience rather than the images about the period received later and from elsewhere. For example, it is a common experience for interviewers to be told that mother did not work; 'Women didn't go out to work in them days.' being fairly typical. But once asked about the daily routine of getting up, going to school, having lunch and so on through the myriad of activities which compose daily life, the fact that as children they got themselves off to school on their own on certain mornings because 'Mum used to do a cleaning job' emerges to contradict their earlier generalization. Another common statement which is proved false with equal frequency is the idea that 'Men did not do housework in those days'. It is these generalized answers to lines of inquiry which reinforce the value of a good detailed schedule. It would appear fruitless to ask if their father helped with the washing-up or cleaning once one has been told that men did not do housework; but informants who have only moments before stated that men did not help in the house will describe how their fathers would wash-up and do various other chores when asked a direct question. One advantage of a list of questions is that it obliges both the informant and the interviewer to proceed beyond their own expectations and preconceptions. For example, an interviewer who shared the assumption that women did not work outside the home and men did not work in it would tend to feel that the truth had been confirmed by the initial generalized answer and to leave the subject. This is where a series of carefully thought-out questions designed to elicit who did what in the daily routine can lead to a more authentic recall of events.

But not even direct questions of detail in isolation necessarily stimulate authentic recall. In this example, early direct questions to the interviewee on whether his mother worked are responded to first with a simple negative, which is expanded with a rational explanation when prompted about part-time work; and it is only some forty pages of typescript later (during a second interview) that he mentions his mother working:

Did your mother work after she got married?

No.

No part-time jobs?

No. She hadn't – looking after a tribe of youngsters [10]. Oh no, was no question of mother going to work. [page 4] . . .

Did your mother have any interests outside the home?

No. Nothing whatever. Well, I'll tell you one thing, when father was out of work you see, everything that was pawnable was pawned. And mother used to go out washing. And it used to be half a crown a day from about eight in the morning 'till six and seven at night. [page 44].[4]

Now arguably he did not think of his mother working in the early part of the interview because she did it only on the occasions when his father was unemployed, but the question about his mother having interests outside the home triggered memories of days when she was out of it. As with the following example, once again a personal explanation, in that her father did not want his wife to work, and a social one, in that it was not the custom, are again proved false well into the interview:

> *Did your mother work after marriage?*
>
> No. My father was rather inclined to be independent and he wouldn't allow her to work you see. It wasn't done in those days you see. Women did not go to work. [page 6].
>
> . . .
>
> In West Norwood my parents had a shop. A sweetshop she – they – my mother used to make all her own sweets. She had the sweetshop, my father was still at work. When he came home he used to help her make the sweets by pulling the sugar over the hook on the door you see. . . . Oh, I'd be what – about – ten probably. . . . We lived at the back of the shop. [page 49].[5]

My experience leads me to believe that the denial of mothers working is more a question of language and communication than one of faulty recall or any form of suppression. In the right context people are quite able to relate what their mothers did. Many people appear to equate questions about work or jobs in the sense of a regular occupation and even prompting about part-time employment does not always elicit the information. That it is revealed in another context – that of being out of the house, or of the houses and locations they lived in – demonstrates the value of prompting for detail, of building up the recall of actual situations and through that giving the informant the stimulus that memories so often need. In most cases a detailed question will bring an appropriate response, and being detailed across a wide area of experience simply makes it more likely that any misremembering in one area will be corrected in another.

One of the arts of interviewing is to be able to ask this amount of detail while encouraging the informants to talk about their experiences in their own words and in their own way. But, as there is no natural law of convergence of interest or a common assumption of what is worth relating, non-directive interviewing will not achieve this aim. Even those who are willing to talk openly about their lives rarely do so in the amount of detail which is needed to create a good historical source. It is the researcher's task to ensure that this takes place and often the questioning and probing for more details conveys a sense of purpose and reassures the informant that the interview is worthwhile. I have been aware in a number of interviews that informants were actively trying to understand just what it was I wanted from them. This can be indicated by responding to the informant's account when it moves in the direction one is seeking to go. It is really a learning process encouraged through feedback and reinforcement. If the information is at all relevant one should never simply listen and then move to the next question one had intended to ask; always ask a question relating to what has been said before returning to one's own line of inquiry. This will encourage the informant to volunteer information rather than remain passive. It is fundamentally a process by which the informant learns to what degree of detail and care you hope the subjects will be treated. This approach cannot be written into a questionnaire, but responding with 'That was interesting . . . (and then asking a question related to its substance)', or, 'Were there similar occasions when that sort of thing happened?' or whatever seems appropriate to encourage the informants to elaborate on something they have told you. Indeed, this is a natural conversational approach and the art of good interviewing lies in being able to keep most of the interview conversational while following the various digressions, remembering which questions the flow of information has answered and yet being prepared to question more deeply and precisely when necessary.

For this reason a questionnaire can never be used simply as a series of questions to administer in sequence. Because real experience is interlinked informants will frequently be providing information which is the answer to questions in more than one conceptually distinct area. A common example is the overlap between leisure and religion. For many of the elderly religious organizations were cultural and leisure centres, particularly in their childhood and youth. So in talking about leisure one may well find that much of the information one wanted about the informant's religion has already emerged obliquely. It would be absolutely crass to later ask questions to which one has already taped the answers. For example, listening to an anecdote about leisure in which Sunday School denomination and activities have figured and then inquiring a few minutes later 'What church or chapel did you attend as a child?', simply because that was a question which had been formulated, is not only unnecessary but irritates informants as it implies that you were not really listening. That the informant had raised the subject of religious affiliation in response to a question on leisure would be an opportunity to include a number of questions on religion as a natural conversational response. In any case one should remember what has been said earlier so that, to pursue the example, when one started asking about 'Religion', instead of the rather formal and deadening 'What religious denomination was your father? To what degree was he active in the church?', one would simply wait for a natural break in the existing subject matter and then say conversationally 'Earlier you were telling me about the chapel (or whatever) and how your mum often went with you, did your dad come with you?'

One has to make a sharp distinction between the questionnaire as a means of conceptualizing the historical subject matter and the interview as a means by which that information is conveyed and in which the informants add their own perspective to the research. Even where the informant is unusually passive it would be a mistake to ask the questions as a series of topics on 'religion', 'work', 'leisure' and so on. To continue with religion as an example. If one wanted to know about the level of religious observance one would have questions about whether grace was said at meals, if bedtime prayers were routine, if they had family prayers and so on. But asking them all together may lead to a poor interview. It will not matter where religion played a large part in the informants' lives; they can respond positively to the line of questioning and volunteer more besides. But if religion was not part of their experience they are obliged to respond with a series of negative answers 'No', 'Never', and so on and this will kill an interview. It will even encourage distorted responses, in that no one enjoys being negative and the fact that you keep asking questions about an area of experience implies that you expect it to have been experienced. These remarks can also be applied to any other area of life which may not have featured very widely in their lives and where pursuing a number of consecutive questions can make people feel inadequate. Nevertheless, the questions need to be asked because one cannot assume, for example, that the family did not observe religious practices in the home simply because they had little or no connection with organized religion, or that they never said prayers because they never said grace. But the questions should be dispersed and placed in their natural context; for example, it is far better to ask if they said grace at meals while talking about food, whether they said prayers at night in the context of bedtime and to approach Sunday through the context of the weekend as a time free of work and mixed with leisure pursuits. In this manner negative responses come singly within the context of other positive responses and do not emerge as an inquisition on one topic about which the informant has no experience.

Interviewing is one of the most rewarding and interesting forms of research, but it does need preparation to do well. Knowing the questionnaire thoroughly so that the questions are in your head, remembering which parts of which sections an informant has answered while remaining alert to what is being said, how far to probe what is said or whether to let the informant continue, all calls for quite intense concentration. It is always much easier and more successful to have two meetings as the first interview can then be much more relaxed and exploratory. This has been my practice whenever possible and a second interview within ten to fourteen days seems to be most informative. Usually the informants will comment on the previous interview and what was said and how it has stimulated them to think about the past (even to dream about it), and how they have recalled things which, as one man expressed it, 'I haven't thought about once since the day they happened'. Having prompted recall with the first visit and the nature of one's interest now being clear, the informant will have a greater sense of the purpose of the interview and, having had time for reflection, will often be more confident and forthcoming.

In the first interview (or at the beginning of a single meeting) it is best to be exploratory and to start from a subject which interests the informant. In fact, informants usually have topics they feel to be of interest and will start by volunteering them, which makes an obvious starting point. But it is useful to establish the broad outline of a person's experience as early as possible as this provides the framework for keeping track on the time and movements of an informant's career. For example, the fishermen I interviewed knew of me as somebody interested in the fishing industry and were keyed up to talk about that when I arrived, so we started with their occupational experience and then went back to the earlier period of childhood and domestic life as the interviews proceeded. But from the beginning I would be gaining a wider sense of the informants' circumstances by asking (at appropriate points) if their father was a fisherman too, whether they had always lived in the port, whether they had any occupation before going to sea, and thus be gradually completing the questions of detail, such as the sociological profile, in a naturalistic way.

I would not, however, want to leave the impression that there is something inherently wrong in asking a series of questions. Questions do not inhibit an informant provided they do not dominate the exchange. For example, if an informant has mentioned several occupations and one is confused as to the sequence and duration of them, it can be useful to say, 'I'm a bit confused about how long you worked at these jobs, could you just make it clear for me?' and then try to establish a sequence with dates, even jotting them down on paper if it will help you to interview more successfully. It is important to make sure that the account one has can be related to other information and historical sources. For example, if in talking about their local area or the class structure they refer to 'posh' people, or to 'them and us', it may be abundantly clear how they felt about the class system without it being at all clear who they exclude as 'them' or include as 'us'. Even if they refer to the upper, middle and working classes *their* meaning cannot be assumed. Their class boundaries, the criteria they use for assigning people to class and how important they felt it to be all need to be established: one has to follow up meanings as well as look for fuller descriptions. This is not such a problem when dealing with matters of factual detail as when trying to establish opinions and attitudes held in the past about class and politics, because these are much more confusable with present values and attitudes. Once again this usually means more detail: which types of person or which occupational groups they felt were in which class and similar 'facts' are the simplest means of establishing their social boundaries. In discussing the interview schedule I emphasized the importance of fixing time as an essential element of historical data. Some experience is easily dated and provides no problem – schooling is an example, war experience is another – but adult social and work experiences cover a lifetime and trying to keep to a period is important. I have known elderly informants who, while talking about how they treated their children, stray without blinking into accounts of how they treated their grandchildren. This is not illogical or unreasonable; you have asked about how they raised their children and they are telling you, and it is your job to be aware of the time of such experience. Where there is the slightest doubt about the period one should cause the informant to consider it: 'How old were you then?', 'Was that before or after you moved to the house at X?', 'Was that before or after you married?', or joined the army or whatever marker in the informant's life will establish the period. And as a minor point, although recording allows for most expressions to be obvious to a listener, if a person uses hands to illustrate size this must be verbalized by the interviewer ('Oh, about x inches') otherwise such information is lost.

The circumstances of the interview will affect the type of information given. From my experience of interviewing people in their own homes or at day centres and similar locations I am convinced that interviews are best done at home; the informant is then in command of the social situation and relaxed in the comfort of familiar surroundings. And although I have had a number of excellent interviews with a third party present (usually the spouse) I much prefer to have no one else present. If informants are alone with the interviewer there is absolutely no call to impress others nor to cover up experiences which they know the third party would not like expressed, or that they would not like to express in front of that person. (As, for example, in one interview where a man's wife constantly tried to prevent him from talking about the poverty of their early years and wanted to suppress anything which hinted at standards of living or behaviour which she felt were below the accepted standards of today.) For many reasons kin and friends can all be more inhibiting than the interviewer. Nevertheless, there are arguments which support group interviews as a constructive method in so far as the memories rub against each other and more information comes as a result. This can be useful in special circumstances such as those reported by John Saville, where detailed research was undertaken before the veterans of a particular Hunger March were brought together.[6] There was then a discussion in which the researcher fed into the discussion evidence from contemporary documentary sources while the informants who had participated recalled their parts in those events and enlarged upon the areas which had not been documented. Clearly interviewing elites benefits from this situation, but generally it would be advantageous only for similar special circumstances of very specific events. The process of having people who shared the same occupation or lived in the same community talking together in the hope of stimulating memories has its dangers. Given what is known about group dynamics and the pressures for agreement and conformity I suspect that the less assured members would have their version of events blotted out by the more dominant members. I would argue that one is more liable to collect the full range and variety of experience within a community by interviewing people singly and collating the experiences rather than by interviewing a group and recording its singular version of experience.

The recognition that circumstances have a biasing effect and a desire to gain a variety of experiences has prompted an interest in the influence that different locations and situations has on the interview content, since different locations bring out rather different memories and accounts. The merits of more convivial settings than is customary has been urged – a public house or after dinner – when people are replete with food and drink and in an expansive mood. I would argue that it depends what one wants from the informant. After dinner is a time when the values of wit, humour and interest outweigh the values of authenticity in the relating of a tale. Dramatic contradictions and embellishments are the stock in trade of the amusing talker, and, indeed, a desirable social accomplishment in such a setting. That guests should be amused is a strong social norm but not one designed to serve the interests of authentic history. Talking in pubs is liable to produce similar distortions. It is not the setting for careful accuracy and judicious reflection. On the other hand the sort of stories told can be very revealing of social, cultural and political attitudes and values: remembered jokes, like the pages of humorous magazines, are informative of their period. My reservation is that the circumstances are such that the social situation of the here and now makes it unlikely that one could safely interpret these accounts as illuminating the past. Formality in interviews has been criticized and the desire to interview groups in convivial settings stems partly from the desire to break down formality – as if the informal were some guarantor of truth and authenticity. The fact that an interview is conducted between two people in private as a formal attempt to collect information does not mean that it need be in any sense unfriendly or tense. It is surprising to read the query 'But how is one to recapture the essential dimension [laughter] through published sources in a formal interview situation, which is by definition a humourless one?'[7] While I would agree that certain types of discourse are less liable in a domestic setting, the jokes and witticisms of an earlier period which indicate values and attitudes are never likely to occur as more than the occasional anecdote in any setting. At least oral history offers the chance to recall and record the humour of an earlier period, and I would be hard pressed to think of a single 'formal' interview where my informant didn't relate amusing incidents and where we didn't share laughter. Most people might be of the opinion that privacy can enhance intimacy rather than the reverse.

Some oral historians have taken this line of approach further and argued that the researcher needs to show a sense of identity or sympathy with a person. This is not a view I share although I would agree that, in general, it would be difficult to sustain a number of interviews with a group of people whose lives, behaviour and values one found totally abhorrent. Nevertheless, I have had good open interviews with people with whom I felt little rapport and had no personal liking. There is even a danger in becoming too intimate, for in the role of a professional researcher it is possible to ask questions which in other, more social circumstances one could not ask. In normal social conversation there is a limit on the degree that it is acceptable to 'pry' into someone's background and origins. The degree to which an interview becomes a conversation between two acquaintances is the degree to which the questions and responses are liable to become governed by customary social conventions. Authenticity is often best served by maintaining an atmosphere of professional inquiry. The key to successful interviewing is to convince your informants of the genuineness of your interest in what they have to say and that what they say is of historical importance: in other words to convince them that you are not there simply for a social occasion and a pleasant, rather inconsequential, chat about the old days; but that you are after as full and accurate information about the past as your informant's experience and memory can furnish. To engage the informant in the desire for accuracy is one of the better ways of collecting authentic information; it need not be a dull process, and it is one which I have found fascinating.

My final observation is based entirely on my own experience as an interviewer. My practice was to challenge the informant as little as possible and to accept the information with little comment, which was the accepted wisdom of the day. I would now be inclined to be rather more challenging and to press an informant where their account seemed contradictory or irrational. Unless conflicts of evidence are resolved during the interview they are unlikely to be resolvable later. Although one must always treat one's informants with respect, part of that respect lies in treating them as a person capable of debate and discussion and not as an old oracle whose message cannot be queried. There is no doubt that many informants would respond with vigour to a more discussive style of interviewing. But it is an intrusive approach which would prove unacceptable to many: wrongly handled it could appear as an attempt to change a person's consciousness rather than to understand it. Clearly the degree to which any element of challenge is introduced should depend on the self-confidence of the informant and the researcher, as it would with any normally sensitive social contact.

Part Three   Assessing the Interviews

7 The single interview: documentary confirmation

I want to emphasise that there is not a sharp dichotomy between two kinds of evidence, one personal, subject to value judgements and bias, the other hard and pure. There is at most a continuum; and no evidence should be treated as uncontaminated fact.

In comparing interviews with other sources it is equally important to recognise that all information is retrospective and the only extra problem that we have in historical interviews is that the time span is longer.

Paul Thompson
'Problems of Method in Oral History', *Oral History*, 1, no. 4, p. 4

One should not over-emphasize the methodological uniqueness of oral evidence. The bulk of documentary evidence is retrospective and originally oral. It is certainly affected by bias and distortion every bit as strong as oral history and frequently much stronger. As we are concerned with the authenticity of oral evidence this is not the place for a lengthy critique of other sources. But it is worth noting that many of the problems of authenticity in oral evidence are simply the problems of documentary sources made plain and the value of any source depends, to some degree, on the quality of alternative sources. Newspapers are a basic source of historical information, but those who have been involved in an incident reported in the press will know just how biased or partial those accounts can be. Reports of accidents or dramatic events come from 'eyewitnesses' which may simply be a blanket term for what a reporter gathered from hearsay; it is certainly retrospective, and the informant may be motivated by the hopes of notoriety or gain rather than accuracy. The political bias of newspaper ownership also ensures that, whatever the 'facts' may be, much information has to be written from a particular viewpoint to be acceptable. Being close in time to an event does not ensure greater accuracy, it simply increases the pressures to record it in a certain manner.

My own fishing research furnished two good examples of how even the simplest contemporary documentary data can be fundamentally inaccurate. Every year the parliamentary papers published masses of very detailed fisheries statistics; these included the tonnage of each type of fish caught, which port they were landed at, which area of the sea they were captured in, which month and so on; 'facts' by the ream.[1] As they were not politically or socially sensitive one might assume that they are accurate. In the larger ports these statistics were collected by an official who would come around and 'interview' the skippers in order to record where they had caught the fish, the species and tonnage. It was from this information that the statistics were compiled. This extract is from an interview I had in 1975 with a fisherman talking about the 1920s:

> Where did you get them? Well you always told a lie over that. You never spoke the truth – not about where you'd been catching your fish, if the Fisheries man came round, or the Customs, whichever he was, he used to out with his book and pencil 'Morning skipper. Where have you been?' You'd tell him twenty or thirty mile out, you never spoke the truth on that. No. Because if you went out and found a good living, a good bit of fish, wouldn't you be silly to go and broadcast it. My word, yes. The next day you'd have three parts of the fleet there wouldn't you.[2]

This desire to conceal from other fishermen where the fish were to be found permeated the fishing industry so the contemporary pressure was always to deceive others, and that extended to the collector of statistics. Those pages of carefully printed statistics are simply oral lies written down by contemporary officials. It takes distance from the events for the authentic story to be related by the original source of such documentary facts. If, in this case, one must choose between the truth of the contemporary or the retrospective I know which I find the most convincing. In the smaller ports this official was only part-time and another informant actually was the collector of statistics for his own port in the 1950s although also a working fisherman:

> I was responsible for all the statistics you know, the amount of fish that was being landed in this place, the value of 'em and all the rest sort of thing. I used to send the returns to London to the Ministry of Agriculture and Fisheries every month . . . I mean what I did report at the end was – they were fictitious figures. For the simple reason, the blokes as I've just explained, if I were to go round and say 'How much have you earned this month John?' well, he wouldn't tell me would he, he'd tell me something but he wouldn't tell me the truth.[3]

Quite simply, by this date, the fishermen were afraid that if they gave full and proper returns on the amount of fish that they had caught to the Ministry of Agriculture and Fisheries they would have to declare earnings for an equivalent amount on their income tax forms. So even 'hard' contemporary statistical data is only what somebody told somebody and if they have good reason and the opportunity to conceal the truth then the 'facts' will be erroneous. Granted the direction of the bias can sometimes be assumed even if it cannot be quantified; few self-employed will over-estimate their income or under-estimate their expenses when filling in their tax forms, although one might assume that a substantial proportion might be tempted to the reverse procedure.

The main issue here is not whether documents are true or false (obviously like interviews some are more accurate than others) but how they serve to confirm or deny the evidence of oral history. And to anticipate the argument, I feel that it is less a matter of testing one source against the other than of being aware of the shortcomings of both and using them as complementary sources to illuminate one another. But where the oral source disagrees with the existing historical accounts established from contemporary documentary sources there is no reason to assume that it is the retrospective oral account which is unauthentic.

Take the very basic 'facts' of census data; they provide as accurate a picture of the distribution of population as one can obtain and it is the sort of information which oral evidence cannot produce. Census data reveals *distributions* but it tells us little about the *motives* of the immigrants nor the social network through which migration takes place.[4] For example, the census will show the number of people in each location, their occupations, how many were born elsewhere and so on. The census data of the place of birth can be used to analyse the pattern and quantity of internal migration and provide a national picture. But oral evidence is better for illustrating the *process* of immigration by providing an insight into individual motives and the social network which leads immigrants to go to particular areas and/or occupations. One of my Norfolk informants related the social process through which five of his siblings migrated to Lancashire. This was all due to the fact that his eldest sister married a railwayman who was moved to Lancashire, and as the younger brothers and sisters left school they went to stay with their sister while they found jobs in the higher paid industries of that area. Motives for much migration are usually expressed as positive economic (pull) factors, as was the motive in this case; life history can reveal the personal factors which determine which people migrate to which location and the earlier experiences which push particular individuals into migrating while others stay.[5] The census, too, shows only the distribution of the population on a given day. Because of this the English census returns under-record anything up to half the number of Norfolk and Suffolk fishermen, simply because at the time of the census the fishermen were working from West Country ports. If recorded at all, they simply inflate the county totals for Devon and Cornwall. So although the census may have a high general level of accuracy the method is too static to record the real distribution of a mobile group such as fishermen and is extremely misleading as to their real home locations. The great strength of oral evidence is that it is dynamic: the census tells us that there are so many fishermen in one place and so many in another on that day; oral histories tell us why they were there, which ones were able to go and that they were at the census location for only eight weeks of the fifty-two.

Documentary sources and oral evidence rarely give direct confirmation of each other if only because the nature of the evidence recorded is rather different. For instance, one informant related her experience of witnessing 'rough music' as a child:

> Well – a long story. 1910 this was. This woman wanted her husband to get away to sea or be earning some money, they'd none. Well, you could understand the woman being – getting on to him about getting off – at the same time, if he couldn't he couldn't. He went on the beach one day, and he was last seen at an angle – I was thinking about that when we, when I was talking about being on the beach, on the hills – and he went, as people saw him, to the south. But he was artful. When he knew people were all down home after their dinners he turned and went north. They ransacked the hills, they went to Yarmouth to see if he went on a boat – and nobody found him. No one. And they gave it up. Well, his poor wife – didn't – hardly get – well she didn't go out of doors. Her mother lived next door to her, and her brother. The result was, a man one evening – this happened in the May, and six weeks following, so that'd be in June, perhaps the forepart of July, I won't say exactly – a man was, well like they used to go walking along the water's edge, and if they see anything they got it, coming ashore. But I don't know if he went for that purpose, he had a dog with him, perhaps he'd come out to give this dog a good run. And this dog *would not* leave this place. That got up in the hills and he kept barking and a-yapping, barking and a-yapping, a good way from Winterton towards the north.

And he thought to himself, whatever on the earth is that – and he called him several times. The result was he had to go and see – and there was this here man tied to a post, about that high, and he – well – he was picked by the birds. Awful. Weren't fit to look at. Of course he got the dog away, when he knew, the dog knew, his master knew what it was he was off. He didn't mind then. Well he had to come home to Winterton and got the coastguard and – report it. And of course there was soon a, well, hullaballoo. There was some people were against her, so much – as if – they dressed up an effigy, lit it up, didn't do it 'til it got dark at night, ten or eleven o'clock, and went round against where they lived. I don't know what they sung now, I was only ten, I forget. In fact, when my mother knew what was going on she came after us. She wouldn't have us be where that was going on. So we came home. But that poor old girl went – well she didn't go mad, but she had to go to the hospital, so she died there.

People felt she'd driven, nagged him into it?

Yes. Yes.

You said it happened in 1910, and you just said you were ten years old.

Well I was ten years old.

If you were ten that would be 1900.

Well, didn't I tell you 1900?

I think that you said 1910.

Ah well 1900 might be, just into the twentieth century. That was June, May when he done it, and I can't tell you the exact date but he was buried in Winterton churchyard. After tea one night. And that was the only thing I ever knew.[6]

He had committed suicide by the extraordinary means of driving a stake into the ground and hanging himself from that. Now clearly such a bizarre event must have attracted the attention of the coroner and the local press. The newspaper reports of the coroner's inquiry confirms the accuracy of her recall (her eleventh birthday was later in the year, so she was ten at this point in 1901); but it does not mention the subsequent 'rough music', and given it happened in a remote village in 1901 there is no reason to expect the reporter of a weekly local paper to be there. So the really interesting part of the oral evidence for social historians, which is the survival of the practice of rough music into the twentieth century, remains without direct documentary confirmation. But I am certain that this is a 'silence' in the documentary record not a phantasy of memory.

The same woman also related a story about the General Election campaign of 1906, and in the course of her anecdote she states that it was '. . . February or March time . . .' and it is clear from the circumstantial detail of her story that she dates this from her memory of the condition of the countryside and that it was dark early in the evening. The local newspaper states that the campaign took place in January and early February, so confirming the general accuracy of her memory. Naturally, however, if one wanted to trace the political activity of an area one would turn to the local newspaper as the first source of information as this is almost certain to have recorded meetings and speakers with an accuracy and detail which oral evidence taken some seventy years after the event could not match. But once again there is nothing to confirm or deny the substance of her story, the point of which for her was that she and a girl friend of the same age were cheeky to the wife of one of the speakers who asked them for directions. But perhaps the main interest in her anecdote for the social historian is that her friend and herself, both aged sixteen, were not allowed to go into the hall and attend the meeting. The exclusion of young women from this form of public activity is unlikely to appear in a contemporary account by a local reporter because he would take it for granted and not consider it newsworthy. She also related how, as they were excluded from the meeting, they spent the evening until nearly ten o'clock, when it ended, going for a walk along the country lanes, which again indicates how women of that age and class spent some of their leisure in a rural location.[7]

So even where there is some congruence with documentary evidence the oral evidence rarely covers the same ground or illuminates the same area of historical interest. Oral evidence not only adds to our understanding of documents, but occasionally illuminates how people used them. For example, many activities are regulated by minimum or maximum ages, such as leaving school, joining the forces and so on. Our birth certificate is the document which excludes us from, or includes us in, various possible activities. One London woman I interviewed[8] related how only about half of her siblings survived infancy and showed me birth certificates to demonstrate that the next child of that sex was christened with the same names. She claimed that this was a deliberate ploy to give flexibility within these regulations. With two birth certificates containing the same particulars they could suddenly be that much older if it suited them for any reason. She claimed that this was a fairly widespread and deliberate policy among the turn of the century London working-class. Whether her generalization from the practices of her own family is correct or not is difficult to assess, but there is no reason why her account of her direct experience should be doubted. Much oral evidence on social practices has to stand alone but should not be doubted simply because it is unexpected. One informant[9] who appeared to have an unusually detailed memory told me how as a ten year old boy he and some friends had bought miniature revolvers complete with ammunition and how he had used his to fire at one of the large glass jars in a sweetshop. I was left for a long time with a very uncomfortable feeling: I was convinced that the bulk of his account was unusually authentic, but how could I justify continuing to believe so when he gave equal conviction to a story I hesitated to accept? It was only some months later that I happened across reports in the local paper of that period recording a number of shootings (including one death) by schoolboys playing with miniature revolvers. I very much doubt whether my eye would have picked up that story as I scanned the newspaper for other information but for my informant. That was unusually fortuitous but it shows that it is dangerous to assume that a piece of oral evidence is exaggerated or imagined just because it does not fit with one's 'knowledge' of the period.

Any evidence is, of course, good or bad only in relation to the use to which it is put. Those who want to use oral history for the precise dating of events, the details of decision making and the generation of policies tend to be most dismissive of its value – while still expending a considerable amount of effort in using it. The failure of elite historians to value oral evidence higher is, to some extent, due to their rather casual methods of collection summed up in the expression 'remembered conversation'. One cannot divorce the value of a source from the method of its creation and were they more rigorous they might obtain more satisfactory results. Nevertheless, they are a difficult group to interview and the chronology and detail of developments and decisions must become blurred in the memories of public figures by the sheer number of debates, committees and so on in which they have been involved. It is not surprising that historians of elites and the biographers of public figures generally find such interviews factually unreliable:

> The near-unanimity among professional authors and historians as to the unreliability of memory to produce information of sequence and hard fact (dates, names, places, etc.) would indeed suggest that oral

evidence should not be relied upon at all for the former, and for the latter only where there are gaps in available written documentation, and where the information can be rigorously cross-checked with other sources for accuracy.[10]

As I have noted earlier, elite interviewing is a particularly difficult genre because of the many people interviewed – politicians, industrialists, trade union leaders – have spent much of their life dealing with interviewers who are trying to discover their intentions, plans and policies and the informants have become adept at giving long answers which say little and of detecting the implications of a question and keeping to a consistent, but not necessarily honest line of answers. In other words they are exceptionally self-conscious of what is revealed in an interview and practised at revealing only that which serves their immediate purpose. There are other elites – creative artists for example – for whom those strictures would not hold to the same degree, but even here the desire to project a particular image may cause distortion. Nevertheless, in an interesting article on elite interviewing Harrison recognizes the difficulties but urges:

> It is probably worth braving the dangers of the interview if one wishes to understand the world of the British politician. The informant may well possess an almost instinctive knowledge of the customs, patterns of behaviour, traditions and ways of proceeding which are so generally accepted within that world that they need never be mentioned in documents sent from one initiate to another.[11]

These aspects are of crucial importance as it is through the culture of political life (or any other milieu) that the significance of a document can be properly evaluated. Not only that, so many documents are written in a formalized style and vocabulary which the historian may need decoded by an insider. Also the mood, attitude and real intent of the writer does not appear in the document but may well be clearly remembered by the writer or colleagues. The mood of politicians, their personal likes and dislikes, rivalries and loyalties are part of the political process and are available to the historian mainly through oral evidence or personal documents. Harrison goes on to argue that far from inhibiting recollection the interviewer is sometimes given information that the informants would not have shared with their contemporaries and peers:

> Indeed, the outsider, by the very fact of exclusion, may receive confidences denied to those inside it. Asa Briggs points out that 'a very

young man . . . can get a lot from a very old man that members of his own generation don't get'.[12]

The idea that an interviewer somehow inhibits confidences is simply not supported by experience, for if written memoirs are a form of oral history set down to mislead historians, as A. J. P. Taylor has claimed, then the advantage of an interview is precisely that it is not a written memoir and that the informant can be questioned on issues which they have not volunteered in memoirs, nor for that matter, confided to their diary, expressed in letters, or which are still secret documents. Although one might also observe that even the most factual and apparently reliable documents can be quite false. Butterfield records how Attlee was obliged to admit to the House of Commons that the defeated British commanders of our failed defences of Greece and Singapore were going to be allowed to rewrite their dispatches before they were published. I have no idea how often that sort of event is allowed in official documents without parliamentary disclosure but it does reveal how far officialdom will go to preserve its own image.[13]

The limitation of so much documentary evidence is that it has been generated by administrative and official processes. What survives is often best suited to administrative and political history – through Hansard, for example, we have a full record of the most insignificant parliamentary debates. Even where the material illuminates social history it remains overwhelmingly the record of formal organizations. This is evident in labour history where unorganized workers do not leave trade union records to provide a source of information, and unless they have been the subject of an inquiry there may be little evidence on which to base a sustained account. These limitations apply even to much local history where the activities of the local sports clubs, Womens Institutes and similar formal organizations will be recorded in the local newspaper although the majority of the inhabitants would not have been participants in those activities, while the local public houses and informal activities which comprised the recreation for far more people will rarely appear.

The strength of oral history is that it can recapture the actual activities of people who never voluntarily participated in formal organizations. It can attempt to record any aspects of life which the researcher feels will be of historical interest and are still within living memory.

The essential point is that one form of evidence can be eloquent
and informative where the other is silent; documentary and oral
evidence are more frequently complementary than contradictory.
For this reason documents cannot be privileged simply because
they are contemporaneous with events. It would be as shortsighted
to write a historical account from contemporary documents alone
where oral evidence is available as it would to write it solely from
the oral – or for either to ignore visual representations of the period
or material remains. But from now on, the memories of hundreds of
people have been recorded and are in archives, future historians
will have access to oral evidence collected before and beyond the
memories of their own epoch's span of living memory. If these
individual testimonies are to realize their full potential as a source of
historical interpretation they must be aggregated to provide a social
interpretation rather than remain at the level of biography.

8 The single interview: internal consistency

> This question of '*historical truth*' can be approached quite pragmatically, as is typically the case in oral history. Here, autobiographical accounts are held to be one data source among several, and to be checked against all other available sources. . . . A more ambitious project is to construct a 'theory of bias' in autobiographical accounts, so that this bias could then be routinely 'discounted' in interpreting such material.
>
> Martin Kohli
> 'Biography: Account, Text, Method', in Bertaux (ed.): 1981, pp. 61–76

The debate on the status of personal reminiscences and whether it is possible to detect and evaluate bias in a systematic way has been developed mainly in relation to printed autobiography. As a life story interview has some similarities with autobiography many of the same questions are of interest to oral historians. I agree with Kohli's view that, in general, the 'truth' of oral history interviews can be judged and used pragmatically. By this I mean by the usual process of triangulating the evidence from one interview with other sources of evidence and with other interviews from informants in similar locations. Nevertheless, as the previous chapter argued that oral history is the only extensive source for large areas of history, so the intrinsic validity of a single testimony is of considerable import.

The dimension which most separates autobiographies from interview life histories is that autobiographers have to be largely self-selecting and self-motivated. Although some people write their autobiographies without intending them for publication most are produced with a readership in mind even if this is only to be their children or grandchildren. The nature of the intended readership will influence, control and limit what the author will be willing to write about which subjects. If one takes autobiographies which have been published or which were intended for publication as being those most readily available as historical sources, the self-willed activity becomes heavily circumscribed by economic and social as well as cultural factors. The current laws of libel will affect what can be written even if it is true; publishers expect a reasonable financial return, so this entails an account which is judged to be interesting enough to extract money from several thousand members of the public; and given our social definitions about what is interesting and significant enough to merit a book (a cultural factor which changes through time) not all types of experience find their way into print. For these reasons the overwhelming number of autobiographies have come from public figures, be they famous or notorious. Those of that genre who rose from working-class backgrounds can display in such titles as *From Crow-Scaring to Westminster* an air of 'rags to riches' which reveals the atypicality of their achievement.[1] Although recent research has revealed the existence of a number of little known working-class autobiographies they are still comparatively rare. Unless they were written by 'leaders' most other working-class autobiographies emphasized the unusual, dramatic or pathetic rather than 'ordinary' life; although, given the tastes of middle-class urban readership, autobiographies which satisfy a taste for rural nostalgia through accounts of bygone 'idyllic' country life appear eternally publishable.

There is also the issue of motivation. People write their auto-biography for various reasons: to justify a public career, because they believe their life exceptional, for immortality, for money, for notoriety, to record a lost way of life, or as a subjective reflection upon their own development and identity. The motive will influence what is written and its authenticity as historical evidence. Apart from those considerations, writing a lengthy script calls for a perspective on writing and books which is most common in the upper and some of the middle classes: it is they, who through occupying more of the elite positions, are self-confident enough to assume that their life is of public interest, or feel the need to account for their custodianship.

In other words, given the cultural definitions and personal perspectives which combine to produce autobiographies it is not surprising that they are biased in content and drawn overwhelmingly from certain types of social experience. What is available to the historical record through published autobiography is limited and unrepresentative simply because it is determined by a complex web of economic, social and cultural power. Oral accounts cannot stand outside those power dimensions and must be affected by them. It is perhaps a reflection of the power structure in our society that the Imperial War Museum, appears to be the institution with the most secure and generous funding for oral history work outside the National Sound Archive itself. In the long term the use made of oral history recordings will largely depend on the amount of funding and institutional support given to making them accessible. Unless they are as readily available as documents are in Record Offices and similar archives then their full potential will not be realized. Oral history practice is, however, not restricted to either institutions or professional elites; compared with producing books it is relatively inexpensive, so it has the potential to reflect a comprehensive diversity of historical experience. It does not rely on self-confident individuals with the time, determination and literary skills to record a particular slice of historical experience. As long as some other person or group is motivated to seek out individuals willing to spend a few hours in conversation the experience of the most diffident, powerless and illiterate can enter the historical record. In this it is more democratic and demotic than written means of recording personal experience, because all social groups can voice their experience in their own words. This at least avoids the sampling bias which limits autobiography as a historical source.

But even if one places to one side the economic and class factors controlling the production of autobiography and accept that they are less intrusive (although not absent) in the production of interview life histories, there is still the issue of how personality will affect presentation and authenticity. Similar questions can be asked about an interview that might be asked of an autobiography. Why have these people agreed to be interviewed? How are they presenting themselves. From what point of view are they relating their life? In earlier chapters we noted that interviewing is affected by who, how and where it is conducted. But these present questions raise the prospect of another form of bias inherent in the character and motivation of the informant in agreeing to be interviewed. A variety of perspectives from which informants might present their life story have been identified: 1) 'rags to riches', a record of their personal success in life; 2) 'nostalgia', they like to reminisce; 3) 'unusual life', they believe their experience to be exceptional; 4) 'loneliness', they simply appreciate a visitor; 5) 'helpful', they want to make a social contribution or do a service to an individual; 6) 'prestige', it flatters their sense of self-importance. These effects have been written about elsewhere[2] and my own feeling is that these factors will not bias an oral history interview as much as they might bias other personal documents. Much of the analysis of autobiography is taken from the standpoint of literary theory and psychology and concerned with the individual and what it reveals of his or her personality. Biography is mainly a form used by elites and they are more self-conscious of their public image and how to present themselves. Indeed biography has been critically identified as a bourgeois form in which the authors 'thematize' their experiences in a manner somewhat akin to the traditional novel form with its self-directing hero. It is easy for elites to view themselves in those terms. It is not so natural to one of the masses.

Working-class informants do not, on the whole, see their lives in a thematized way as the theory of bias would suggest everyone must do. When they do it is usually along a simple and straightforward lines of 'I have always worked hard' or 'Been honest' or 'Willing to help another' and there is no doubt that such a self-image will form a 'routine bias' in their account, and that many events and activities will be told in relation to that theme. But it is still not clear to me how to distinguish between a subjective 'thematization' (which it is assumed will bias an account) and a 'principle' of conduct which has actually shaped the behaviour and values of a lifetime. In any case, although interviewing produces a memoir of the person it is not an 'auto-' anything, it is not a product of the individual, it is a social enterprise. The informants are not left to write what they will and ignore what they wish, they are prompted into describing and explaining aspects of their experience which they would not have described, with details they would not have considered worth recording. Perhaps even more crucially they are people who would not have considered the possibility of any form of autobiography. Whatever 'bias' informants might have set down if writing their life is constantly disrupted by the intervention of the researcher: the fact that oral history is a joint enterprise does make it less prone to a display of individualistic thematizing.

Nevertheless, personalities vary. While some people are boastful and will exaggerate their role in any event, others are retiring and will understate their contribution: personal accounts through interviews are not simple mirror-images of truth. Informants' self-images will affect which aspects of their life they will spontaneously volunteer. For example, one man I met graphically related the first three years of his working life with very little intervention or prompting; yet the subsequent fifty–four years of his working life were related in as brief a space and much of that was curt answers to my direct questions. There is a distinct difference between the enthusiasm with which he talked about his three years during which he had a variety of occupations and his lack of interest in talking of his long years in one firm. This proportion seems to reflect a real bias rooted in his personality and significant for how he wanted to be seen. He undoubtedly had an image of himself as a rather adventurous young man who 'knocked about a bit' and one who remained a 'bit of a card'. His account is most probably systematically biased – wherever possible – to support this image. But the significant *historical* factor is that he was a secure employee of a paternalistic firm. His industrial, social and political activities are therefore illuminating for that category of worker rather than for the 'rolling stone' of his imagination.[3]

In spite of this some interviewers place a high value on information given spontaneously because they believe that when informants volunteer information they relate what is significant in their lives. What is salient to the informant is assumed to have a greater authenticity than responses to the interviewer's questions. Certainly one always encourages people to volunteer information but what they say cannot be granted a privileged status: one cannot assume a congruence between the willingness to volunteer information and that information being the most salient aspect of that person's life. Indeed, in my view, they themselves may volunteer some information because they assume it is the sort of thing a researcher would most want to know, or because they feel that they are the most dramatic, impressive events to a stranger, or give them a role in national events. In any case what is most salient to the informant for whatever reason is not necessarily the most significant in terms of historical (as opposed to biographical) research. In the example given above the informant wanted to project a more varied image of his life than his experience actually warranted. Without a fairly controlled interview one could easily have been left with the impression of a variety of jobs lasting much longer than they did. If an awareness of such personality bias is to help in a more rigorous analysis of oral history its greatest value might lie mainly in detecting this early in the interview(s). One then might be in a position to try to gain their explanation as to why they stayed so long in one occupation when they appeared to have enjoyed and valued change – rather than merely being aware of this aspect after the interview is over.

The largest bias may well be in what is left unsaid rather than what is said. There is no point in believing that any source of history is complete: history has always been written from fragmentary sources so this is no new thing. Clearly few, if any, interviews will ever cover all aspects of an informant's life, and what is not discussed is left as missing information. The important thing is to conduct interviews so that it is apparent whether information is missing because the informants avoided answering questions or gave undue prominence to other aspects of their lives. This would not be so important if individual informants avoided relating certain particular incidents in their lives – no one is liable to tell all – but it would be of historical significance if all informants were systematically silent on particular areas of public experience. The idea of silences arose from research into the fascist period in Italy where it was observed that informants skipped the period of fascist rule when volunteering an account of their lives; the argument being that there are public and national events which impose a silence on those who participated. In other words memory – or at least oral history – is constrained and constructed by social rather than by individual factors. This is an aspect I shall leave for a closer consideration in Chapter 11 on memory, as the notion of 'silences' in people's testimony has been developed within the model of memory and its relationship to the social and political structure.

At a recent oral history conference it was suggested that oral historians should adopt a code of conduct which, although it would not avoid bias, would go some way to ensuring that the authenticity of the evidence could be evaluated. This code states that the tapes should always be preserved without editing so their bias of questions, emphasis, irony and so on is apparent; and the time, place and circumstances of the interview should be noted as well as who else was present. With these details and the original tapes any shortcomings in the interview can be known – for example, just which subjects they avoided (silences), or which ambiguities were left unexplored, and the degree of conviction and certainty in the informant's voice. The accent itself is historical evidence, particularly in England where it is such a significant marker of status. One researcher has observed how the women from a small Essex town who had worked as shop assistants had a more refined accent than women who had not – and this was confirmatory evidence for the pressures of occupation and class.[4] Changed speech is a result partly of environment but also of conscious desire. One domestic servant I interviewed, who asked to hear herself on tape, was very shocked because she felt that her voice sounded 'common' and was convinced that after all her years as a lady's maid her voice and accent were much more cultured than I had recorded. Nevertheless, whatever the accent, some facets of experience are more personal than others, so people respond with varying degrees of frankness and honesty to various questions. So although it is constructive to be aware that personal and social factors will give a 'bias', I am not aware of any method of 'routinely' discounting such factors. Even psychologists need a little longer and interviews in more depth to understand an individual's self-image – historians might be best advised not to try. But that still leaves the problem of how to evaluate an interview and how much credence to place on it.

As far as I can see this has to be a matter of internal coherence. In other words the interview has to be sociologically and historically convincing as a whole. This reiterates the importance of a questionnaire and the conduct of the interview. These ensure that various interrelating facets of a person's life have been included and it is the coherence of these which provides the basis of internal consistency (for example, where the questions have been thought through and asked, accounts of leisure cross-check with accounts of friendship and kinship networks, just as they cross-reference to accounts of social class and those, in turn, with accounts of standard of living and domestic life). This is not simply a matter of checking 'fact' against 'fact': a rounded interview allows the informant's meanings of words and references to become apparent in a way more cursory methods do not. For example, one informant described her very poor working-class background and yet, when asked a direct question, replied that she was 'middle class'. This made sense only if evaluated within her social framework, for the term obviously did not mean what sociologists or historians or indeed what most people would mean by it. What is said cannot always be simply translated as what is meant in terms of most other people's usage; to evaluate an interview one must enter into the informant's meaning of words. Her meaning was that, as some people were better off than her family and some were worse off, they themselves were (quite logically) 'middle' class. She placed very few others, virtually only vagrants, below herself, but owing to her unusually limited social horizons she placed even corner shopkeepers into the upper class, so by her criteria 'middle' actually refers to 'manual working class'. But it is only through a thorough description of her life and values that one can be certain that this claim to be middle class was not due to the status inflation so frequently postulated by sociological surveys. The value of consistent interviewing is precisely that it can reveal contradictions through collecting the detail which any historian will need in order to understand generalized comments. Even where values and attitudes are not expressed overtly it is often possible to assess these from the nature of the daily round and how it was experienced. This is not a process of piling positivistic fact on fact but a process of gaining sufficient specific references for the denotation and connotation of the informant's vocabulary to be properly understood.

When asked to talk about certain areas of their life, especially relating to childhood, informants will, not unnaturally perhaps, speak with a great deal of certainty and confidence which is a barrier to distortion. This is not present when the interviewer is trying to elicit the informants' accounts of the class structure of their local community in terms of the class structure as understood by social scientists. Informants may not have formalized their social experience into a consistent and easily articulated pattern, and where the informants are least clear in their own minds how to express themselves in a way which the interviewer can comprehend they are most liable to accept the vocabulary and divisions offered them by the interviewer. Thus there is a minimum danger of miscommunication when someone is discoursing fluently and a maximum danger when they are borrowing from the vocabulary of their interviewer. Just occasionally the vocabulary of the informant is exciting in so far as it appears to signal a reimmersion in an actual period as the informant slips into phraseology which is no longer current. For example, Bernard Waites has examined the imagery and language of class in the period 1900 to 1925 and found that:

> . . . the 'submerged tenth' and 'the upper ten', which were common parlance before 1914 for the extremes of poverty and wealth, fell out of use with the eradication of much of the primary poverty of Edwardian England and the inroads to some of its conspicuous wealth.[5]

Yet in two of the East Anglian interviews I conducted in the mid-1970s just such a phrase occurs quite naturally as a description of class. The first occurred while I was asking about the Church of England's congregation: 'Well, they were more like the upper ten, what we called the upper ten really. Farmers, farmers wives and – that sort of people – the butcher.' That informant was born in 1886 and was describing the village of Kessingland in Suffolk prior to 1914. He has adapted the terminology to the social structure of his locality, but it is expressed with a certain self-conscious irony. The other example, from West Mersea, Essex, comes from an informant not born until 1900. This emerged during a discussion of politics in the 1920s when I asked what sort of people were Conservatives: 'Well, all the farmers and the – what you'd call the upper ten was Conservatives.'[6] This example appears to refer to the national class structure and reflects the social experience of the fishermen from this area. They worked during the summer as crewmen on the luxury sailing yachts of the period and so were familiar with members of the national elite as their employers. In both cases, however, one feels that the language itself adds to the authenticity of the information.

It has been claimed that life history records are the most perfect type of sociological document because all other records are only fragments of experience and, therefore, have a less complete context; the greater the context of a piece of information the more complete its meaning. Certainly the completeness of 'context' in an extensive interview is one of its major guarantees of authenticity. The specific context of daily routine must carry more weight than a brief response to a single question however apparently certain that may be (as in, for example, those cases where the informant gives a confident 'no' to the question of whether their mother worked outside the home and then, in recalling the daily routine, gives a number of specific instances which contradict their earlier denial). Ostensibly one has a contradiction in the interview but the detailed 'context' leaves no doubt as to which answer is to be believed.

There is a problem where informants do not distinguish between direct personal experience and information they know from other sources. I once interviewed a man whose description of work left me doubting the veracity of his account. It seemed rather non-specific and slightly anachronistic. Eventually he asked me if I knew a book called *The Ragged Trousered Philanthropists*. It was then quite clear that he was relating what he had read there as responses to my questions about his experience in the building trade. This was not, in my opinion, from any desire to deceive: I had told him that I wanted to know what the building trade used to be like and he was obliging by telling me what he knew. Indeed, he implied that I was wasting my time because it had already been recorded in that book.[8] Let me make quite clear that I am not objecting to informants passing on information other than direct experience. The problem is simply that if we cannot distinguish between their primary experience and secondary knowledge then the authenticity of the resulting amalgam of information cannot be easily established in terms of provenance and dating. An essential part of the specific value of oral history depends on being able to identify direct experience, as the informant's age and location is the essential guarantor of provenance. Unless the process of creating the interviews discussed in Part Two is rigorous enough to reveal the distinction between 'directly experienced' and the 'learned about' then the ultimate authenticity of the information will be considerably undermined.

In assessing an interview it is also worthwhile to make a clear distinction between *generic* and *specific* information as well as direct experience and learned information; that is, the distinction between the individual's own experience and that of other people such as workmates or neighbours. Many useful comparisons can be had from this distinction. For example, if the informant relates accounts of holidays enjoyed away from home one can be left wondering whether that was typical or exceptional for a person of this occupation, income level or class. As one usually lives in a neighbourhood where people are of much the same class one can ask if that was usual or whether they were exceptional in that regard. For example, in reading a number of working-class oral history interviews I have noticed that low-paid railway workers' children at about the turn of the century enjoyed holidays more frequently than the children of much more highly-paid artisans. The reasons are complex but undoubtedly include the fact that many railwaymen were recruited from country areas and so had relatives to whom the children could be sent for a country holiday; and because they enjoyed concessionary travel they could send them at little cost. Now their recollection of whether *they* had holidays or not is going to be of a more authentic status than their assessment of whether others had similar experience: but their view of their life as being better or worse than those of their contemporaries is obviously invaluable and is located in these contextual details. It can account for otherwise puzzling industrial, social and political attitudes. Our assessments must be based in socio-structural frameworks which suggest that certain patterns of behaviour are likely to be experienced by particular socio-economic groups. This must also be properly historical; people are not only stratified by class or separated by gender, but within those categories are laminated by cohort experience: they leave school, get married, have children and so on at times when the socio-economic structures have a different bearing upon them. Although we are dealing with the experience of individuals the analysis of historical structure and change must remain the focus, and not the individual either as a psychological entity or as a social atom.

9 Aggregating data

When we describe and analyse human society as it existed in the past or as it exists at present, we inevitably make use of numbers and quantities. Age, date of birth, wealth, number of wives, numbers of children – all these are quantitative characteristics of a person which we must discover if we are to give an adequate description of him. In doing this, we measure, compare him with other people, richer or poorer, older or younger, and seek by these means, as well as by discussion of his thoughts and his work, to place him within the society in which he lived.

Roderick Floud
An Introduction to Quantitative Methods for Historians (Methuen 1973)

It is an essential part of the historical discipline to understand how human activity and consciousness change through time, their social locations and the material reality within which they are formed. This can be done only by moving from the individual accounts to social interpretations. Aggregating data from interviews is one such method. Nevertheless, aggregating oral history data has been criticized as being essentially a positivistic 'quantitative' process which is inherently inappropriate to the 'qualitative' insights of oral evidence. Such objections are entirely inappropriate. No matter how often, or by what methods, an interview is analysed the original tapes and typescripts are still there for qualitative use. There is no conflict or question of having to use only one of the alternatives, it is purely a matter of whether aggregating the data is a worthwhile activity in itself. I would argue that it is, and that it is going to be an even more informative procedure as the number of interviews available increases. Indeed, it will become essential because the difficulties of making the maximum valid use of oral evidence will grow as the number and range of interviews archived and available for use increases.

At present many historians simply assume that their informants' experiences are in some sense typical of their group, the group being defined by the historian in terms of the informants' gender, location, occupation or whatever other characteristics define the limits of their particular study. This may not be an unreasonable process of historical analysis where an individual researcher's interviews are related to a single community or occupation, usually chosen to explore a particular facet of experience. Their criteria of selection should ensure that they can generalize with some confidence about the experience of that group. To accept this as the limit of broader analysis open to oral evidence would be to confine it to local and limited studies. But as these particular and individual studies become part of an archive their *collective* potential for new and social and comparative studies increases: the longer that oral history archives are established the wider the spread of birthdates available, so increasing the potential for genuine historical analysis through cohort analysis. But the sheer volume of material means that it becomes too large a source to approach 'qualitatively' in the sense of one researcher reading and digesting all the relevant interviews. As with most sources of historical evidence one will be obliged to approach it through some process of selectivity. To be able to select will require that the basic factsheet information of age, location, occupation and so forth has been coded and indexed. Thus the problem of interpreting oral evidence is linked to issues of archiving and the selective retrieval of information.

Archiving is a specialist skill and its wider aspects go beyond the aims of this book or the competence of its author.[1] There are various types of archive each of which would need their own approach, and, as Margaret Brooks of the Imperial War Museum Sound Archives has written, there is 'no satisfactory extant oral history cataloguing system, although the Imperial War Museum and the Museum Documentation Association are developing models.'[2] Clearly the need for appropriate systems will lead to their development. But archivists are, quite properly, primarily concerned with preserving and indexing their material and not with analysing and interpreting it. The cataloguing systems they develop, therefore, are liable to be geared to those ends. At the moment the Imperial Museum uses the customary factsheet details of date, location, rank, and so forth with the synopsis of the interview as a guide to content. Margaret Brooks writes that the museum's experience suggests that 'A synopsis of fifty to seventy-five words per thirty minutes of recording is appropriate'. She acknowledges, however, the advantages of the more difficult method of 'conceptual indexing' which '. . . creates much more complicated problems for both cataloguer and user but is likely to increase the value of the collection and broaden the range of potential users.' I would agree with her on both the advantages and difficulties of conceptual indexing. It presents particular problems to public archives, such as the National Sound Archive or local record offices, which accept deposits from a variety of sources. This means that the collection comprises separate projects which may have few features in common, so that new deposits may not fit very easily into an existing conceptual scheme formulated for existing holdings.

This difficulty with conceptual indexing need not apply to an archive which pursues its own research projects – as does the Imperial War Museum. Margaret Brooks points to 'continuity' as one clear advantage that institutional archives have over individual research projects and suggests that they could gain better records by interviewing '. . . eminent figures at more than one point in their lives – say, at the ages of 45 and 65, depending always on personal career patterns'. She extends this to those out of office and 'eminent failures'. This would obviously be useful, although many social historians would see no reason why such programmes should not be applied to recording a cross-section of non-elite figures. Nevertheless, she supports the view that 'historical analysis benefits if the interviews are comparable' so confirming my earlier arguments about the need for consistent interviewing. Whatever research role some specialist oral history archives establish for themselves there will still remain a need for local and national institutions to archive interviews from other research projects and private individuals if much good historical material is not to be lost. Some archives will need to accept a variety of material, and will have to make it as accessible as are documents in record offices if historical study is to fully benefit from its content.

Paul Thompson is the British oral historian (as opposed to archivist) who has been instrumental in initiating and pursuing the building of an archive and furthering oral history research and methodology through consistent interviewing and conceptual indexing. His original project *Family Life and Work before 1918* was the basis of the Essex Oral History Archive and the principles which he established are the basis of the methodological practice advocated here.[3] He used a quota sample of 444 informants based on the 1911 census in order to ensure that the research was broadly representative of the social structure of the period. The research was planned to respond to a degree of elementary statistical analysis and to this end a detailed interview schedule was used to ensure that, within the context of an open-ended interview, the same range of topics would be covered with each informant. The interviews were initially indexed by a factsheet card which enabled researchers to find those interviews which related to the area or occupation which interested them. Subsequently the potential for analysis was greatly extended through coding the interviews across a range of variables and entering these into a computer for easy retrieval and manipulation. The interviews were coded to 191 variables for the 444 cases covering information such as gender, date of birth and similar aspects of a sociological profile. Places of residence were coded according to geographical region and according to whether that residence was rural or urban; occupations according to the traditional divisions of unskilled, semi-skilled, skilled as well as by the Registrar-Generals' three-digit codings. These codes obviously enable researchers to select those interviews which contain the type of social experience they require from the region which interests them.

In principle there is no limit to the amount or type of information which one might select for coding; among other things, we coded the number of rooms in the house, whether informants had kin or lodgers living with them; whether father washed-up, did cooking or cleaning, put the children to bed, played with them or took them out; their political or religious affiliations and the degree of involvement. The coding for each piece of data was developed from the amount of detail found in the interviews; sometimes this might only warrant a simple 'Yes', 'No' or 'Don't know', but where there was sufficient information it was further coded on a three-point scale, indicating perhaps the intensity or frequency of an activity (Regular, Occasional, Rare), or on a five-point scale (Very Regular, etc.). Much of the information was descriptively coded according to categories suggested by the nature of the experience. For example, the type of punishment experienced as a child was grouped according to the different means parents used, conceptualized as degrees of increasing severity, whether it was (1) 'Verbal only', (2) 'Restricted playtime or reduced pocket money', (3) 'Rarely corporal' and so on; this type of coding can create as many categories as seems conceptually useful. In fact, the archive interviews have been coded in this particular example through seven categories finishing with the most severe one of 'Frequent harsh corporal'. With these variables it is possible to interrogate the archive to see if there are any major differences in the treatment of children by parents of different occupations, social class or regions, or whether it correlates with family size, the mother working or whatever other dimension that has been coded and appears conceptually interesting.

If the number of categories is too complex they can easily be aggregated into fewer; for example, the seven levels of punishment would be dichotomized into 'corporal' and 'non-corporal' to provide a simpler analysis. However, one should always code the material as widely as possible because complex codings can be simplified but simple codings cannot be made more complex. For example, the number of children in a family ranges from nil to around twenty and this information (and similar) should always be coded raw. It might not be practicable to correlate the use of corporal or non-corporal punishment across nearly twenty categories, but one can construct categories at will such as 'Small families' of 1 to 3 children, 'Medium families' of 4 to 6, and 'Large' of 7 and over. It would be an irretrievable mistake to decide in advance to code the interviews into these three groups however appropriate they may be for one's own research, because once that has happened it is impossible to rearrange the nature of the categories; whereas, if data is coded by the actual number of children one could try changing 'Medium' to include three children, or seven, or both. In other words the greater the range of coding, the greater the possibility to construct categories for different purposes and from different conceptual assumptions.

The great advantage of conceptual coding is that it can be a cumulative process. Researchers use the material for their own research interests and from within their own conceptual framework, but as they work on and code different aspects of the interviews these become available for general analysis with aspects already coded. Not all coding, however, is analytical in intent; some is purely indexical and allows researchers to find those interviews which refer to specific items, thus saving them the task of reading through all the interviews to find whatever (few) references the archive may contain on their subject of interest. Most codings, however, can be used for both retrieval and analysis; for example, 'politics' and 'religion' can be used to simply recall those interviews where the parents or informant were of a particular religious or political affiliation, but can also be used to see if the regularity of attendance or intensity of involvement correlates with any other variable. Conceptual coding can give a very detailed index, as one example will show. Political activity was coded on six points: (1) 'Active' refers to any involvement from addressing envelopes, canvassing and upwards in the electoral process, (2) 'Overt interest' refers to those who attended meetings, displayed posters at their home and so on, (3) 'Voter' is self-explanatory, and one continues through non-voters to the a- and anti-political. Such codings can be grouped or simply dichotomized into voters and non-voters for simple analysis, but they enable a researcher to consult the interviews they really need. For example, one could discover which interviews were with political activists of a given party allegiance in any region. One could also select on the basis of religious affiliation or occupation or whichever criteria one wished to consider. Practically it enables a researcher with limited time to start working on those interviews which are most liable to contain the required information rather than spend days fruitlessly scanning pages of transcripts.

It must be acknowledged that in good open-ended interviews responses are discursive, and coding them is a very subjective process because only a small proportion of the information can be considered unambiguously factual and quantitative. Where values such as class or industrial attitudes are being coded a high degree of the coders' interpretation enters into the process. It is for these reasons that thoughtful and meticulous interviewing is so essential. If an interview has contradictions which are not resolved during the interview then the degree of variation of interpretation is increased. Ideally coding and analysis should go hand in hand with the initial interviewing so that interviewers are aware of where their interviews need to be more detailed or searching. For example, a sector on class attitudes and values proved particularly difficult to structure, code and analyse. This was not from lack of information because most interviews have plenty of material on class through anecdote, allusion and description as well as in response to direct questions. All coding of this sort of information depends to a large degree on the historical sensitivity of the coders and their appreciation of what the informants meant. But practice could be improved by building in markers which each informant is asked. After all, one of the basic interpretative elements is to understand how the informants view the class structure, the number of classes they see and where they draw class boundaries. But one difficulty which became apparent at the coding stage was that some informants had responded to the subject by talking about their own direct experience of class, which is to say in terms of the local visible class structure, whereas others had responded in terms of their concept of the national class structure. There is nothing 'wrong' in the content of either type of response, but those who have discussed class only in terms of their direct contacts and observations of their local community may well have added one or more levels to their perceived hierarchy if they had been asked about class at the national level. Where the national or local level of the material on class has not been made clear any analysis of the relationship between class attitudes based on the comparison of such basic elements as the number of classes and who is included in them becomes rather tenuous. Yet it would not be difficult, nor would it overstructure an open-ended interview, to ensure that some questions are included which ask informants to give their views on class locally and nationally. Indeed, such questions might well prove a catalyst for a more qualitatively informative description of class as well as a more codable one – and the same is true for many other areas of information. Being able to make the greatest authentic use of what informants have said depends on being able to understand their frame of reference with confidence.

The data at Essex is on SPSS which is designed for analysis of synchronic data. For reasons too extensive to rehearse here this was preferred as a first step in coding and analysis to a programme designed for life-history data.[4] It was preferred because it is widely understood, easily learned and suitable for indexing and retrieval while basically designed for the statistical analysis of social science data. It does not handle nominal data such as place names although, of course, these can be entered and retrieved through suitable coding schemes. Or indeed, as we have done, one can enter nominal data in separate files (Cobol) which cross-references to the coded files. Naturally much of this coding is 'conceptual' indexing: one has preconceived notions as to the analytical value of such concepts as 'class', and assumes that the number of classes perceived by a person and the boundaries of those classes are of theoretical importance in explaining behaviour and values. Similarly if one were interested in the division of domestic and paid labour, and how this was shared within families by gender and age, these aspects of the interviews would be coded.

This data has not yet been analysed in any depth, but some distributions taken during the research process suggest that the interviews are a cohesive collection as planned. For example, work experience was coded along a number of dimensions, one of which allows the various workplaces to be grouped as 'Large', 'Medium' and 'Small'. These were then cross-tabulated by location and the resulting distribution is 'typical' in that 42 per cent of the large are found in cities, 33 per cent in towns and 12 per cent in rural areas (the rest were unclassifiable or never worked). Even such a contingent matter as the distribution of trade union membership among the informants reflects historical reality with the lowest reported membership coming from East Anglia and the highest from Lancashire and Cheshire; and when correlated with the size of the workplace 65 per cent of union members were employed in large places of employment and only 15 per cent in small. Even with more subjective data such as whether the individual informants perceived their wages as above or below average, the results, when aggregated, showed 31 per cent perceiving their wages as above average and 24 per cent as being below average, which suggests that the archive has not only collected a cross-section of occupations, but that it has gathered an experience which reflects a social norm. Of those who perceived their wages as being above average 67 per cent felt that their employer was 'good', compared with only 33 per cent perceiving their employer as 'good' who described their wages as below average. This sort of result gives some confidence in the wider 'authenticity' of the interviews *as a collection*. For although it is impossible to establish their validity as a statistically valid sample, examining the 'sample' through such distributions demonstrates that if the social experience in the archive has a distribution which is conformable with what is known from other, contemporary sources, then the archive could be used to make general statements, with some degree of confidence, about those areas where the historical record is inadequate and, given a large enough sample, might be used to suggest some generalization and fruitful lines of further historical inquiry.

The value of this approach will only be established through use and refinement. But the areas which are least well-documented in contemporary sources include domestic life, childhood experiences, and the paid labour of women. If the archive does prove to be 'typical' then even the raw frequency accounts in such other areas must lead to some revision in the general picture where they clash with accepted wisdom. For example, most previous assumptions about child socialization postulate the general use of corporal punishment, but according to the testimony about their own child-hood from the 444 informants computerized at the Essex Archive 32 per cent were never chastised by either parent, and over 50 per cent were never chastised by their fathers; similarly, 30 per cent of the informants report that their fathers would do a certain number of domestic chores such as cooking and cleaning, which undermines many assumptions about the division of domestic labour around the turn of the century and earlier. And here one might note how quickly the value of an oral history archive grows. In the Essex Oral History Archive *Family Life* project of 444 cases, 70 per cent of the informants were born before the twentieth century and 27 per cent on or before 1890. The material in this archive is now irreplaceable and totally unrepeatable – and if a similar archive of interviews with people from all regions and classes existed for any other earlier century it would probably transform our view of the social history of the period.

This process of analysis through coding is most valuable where the interviews have been guided by a schedule which has ensured that everyone was asked for the same range of information. If this has been done then it is possible to make some further analysis. Thus, although the data is not statistically valid, by tabulating it one can see whether it follows convincing patterns which fit known historical trends. The demographic details, for example, can be structured to provide comparisons with what is known about family size and factors affecting mortality. The accompanying tables are taken from my work on the East Anglian fishermen and are intended to show what is gained by analysing a comparatively small project of sixty interviews.[5]

Table A gives the figures for all the interviews, thus providing a baseline of the collective experience as reported by that group of informants from one region and occupation. From what is known about morality in the period the sample would conform to histori-cal patterns if mortality were higher in urban than in rural locations: Table B demonstrates this trend to an unexpected degree given that East Anglian urban areas were comparatively small. Table C divides the group in cohorts by decade of birth and although the trend in sibling mortality is less evenly spread it is in the direction that one would expect. The increase in family size in the final cohort is against the general trend, but as this was a prosperous period for the fishermen it may indicate a real local trend to larger families.

If a group of interviews is conformable to known trends then one

Reported family size and mortality

		Average number of siblings per informant (%)	Reported number of sibling deaths (%)	Sibling mortality (%)	Number of informants
A.	All informants	8.0 (482)	1.0 (58)	12.0	60
B.	Urban	8.0	1.2	15.0	32
	Rural	8.0	0.7	9.0	28
C.	→ 1889	9.6	1.3	14.0	18
	1890–1899	7.0	1.0	14.0	27
	1900–1909	8.0	0.5	7.0	15
D.	Drifting	8.0	1.3	16.0	16
	Trawling	9.4	1.6	17.0	12
	Inshore	6.7	0.5	7.0	20
	Others	8.9	0.8	8.0	12
E.	Owners	8.2	0.8	11.0	9
	Skippers	8.3	1.3	16.0	13
	Crew	9.5	2.3	25.0	6

Table E has only 28 cases because it refers to drifters and trawlers only, as 'inshore' boats were not large enough for status distinctions.

can have some confidence that internal distinctions are liable to reflect real changes in social experience. This assumption is enhanced by Table E. High mortality is associated with poverty and class, so given that there is a structured difference of income within the group this should also be reflected in variations in the mortality rate. This trend shows much more strongly than the qualitative material would suggest. The qualitative evidence, almost without exception, emphasizes the common lot of the fishermen and minimizes the status differences within the community. Any interpretation based solely on the qualitative accounts would miss this very clear pointer to the strength of the distinction this table suggests. Table D is interesting, for it shows something which cannot be known unless data is aggregated. It shows that the families of men engaged in drifting and trawling have similar mortality rates whereas the inshore fishermen and workers ashore (Others) also have very similar but much lower rates. As none of this data is statistically valid and there are other significant factors (the age and location of the informants in each category, for example) the tables can be no more than a suggestive example of the sort of analysis which could be applied to larger numbers. Certainly the evidence appears in a new light if it is structured. One obvious difference emerges from the pattern of work with high mortality where the men were away from home for long periods, and low mortality where the men were at home regularly. This focuses attention on domestic structure and behaviour and queries the view, put forward in some sources, that these working-class males were selfish, brutal engrossers of family resources. Had they been, one would have expected families to have survived better when they were not present rather than the reverse. Simple structuring provides insights which are not possible when the interviews are treated as separate testimonies. For example, the methods of socializing children in the home were also tabulated according to the frequency and severity of corporal punishment and which parent administered it. In this sample only 22 per cent of fathers chastised their children compared with 42 per cent of mothers, which again makes good sense given that it was an occupation which left the women to control their children alone for much of the time. Interestingly enough the pattern was the same as the mortality table in that, although the male behavior did not change much with regard to the proportion of them who chastised their children, the absence of the male from home dramatically increased the use of corporal punishment by women. Thus tabulation obliges one to consider relationships between work patterns, family life and the effect that this has on individual behaviour from perspectives which are not apparent in the qualitative evidence of single interviews.[6]

It must be reiterated, however, that such an analysis is based on the concept of the individual case, the informant's *own* occupational, social and political experience and so on, but interviews are not simple repositories of information restricted to an informant's experience. They also include much information about what the informants observed of the behaviour of the world around them. There appears no practical way of including this information in the analysis, although it could be referenced under a separate coding and indexed for retrieval. The experience of coding a large archive was in itself instructive as it subjected the interviews to an unusually stringent scrutiny. Given that the interviews were collected as a quota sample and used semi-structured interviews, the collection has a greater inbuilt consistency than a public archive established from varied accessions. The high rate of positive coding possible across a whole range of experience testifies to the soundness of this policy. The ability to code and analyse *post hoc* depends on the fullness and rigour with which the interview topics were covered in the first place and missing details can make a difference to the confidence with which information can be used. For example, an interview which has a rich description of a local community including street evangelists, charity visitors, the various religious denominations and their congregations, would be lacking if it failed to elicit the informant's own religion and degree of commitment. That information would be needed for any analysis of the relationship between religious affiliation and any other aspects of the informant's social experience.

Computer analysis also holds the potential to contribute to solving other methodological problems associated with interpreting oral evidence which, so far, have mainly been approached from a qualitative angle. For example, a number of oral historians have reported that men and women recount their experiences differently owing to gender conditioning. This is observed through their form of narrative as well as in the values and attitudes through which they express observed social phenomena. Although these are qualitative assessments it is perhaps only through quantitative analysis that one might understand how extensively gender affects recall of the past and in which areas of experience. It is noticeable that in the *Family Life Project* (216 male and 228 female), women reported a higher level of involvement by their fathers over a series of variables on domestic routine than did the men. Now that may simply be an accident of the sample. However, virtually the only domestic activity of their fathers which men report more frequently than women was their father dressing or undressing them as children. This exception suggests that the reported experience is collectively authentic, as given the greater taboos on touching between male and female, particularly at this historical period, the greater frequency with which fathers helped their sons rather than their daughters might be anticipated. If, for the moment at least, it is accepted that the differential reporting of domestic life generally is due to gender rather than an accident of the sample, then one can begin to speculate as to why this should be so. Lines of interpretation might be that as girls were involved more heavily in domestic chores than boys they remember more clearly which of their parents did domestic labour and to what degree; or that their greater involvement with domestic labour throughout their lives has served to reinforce their memories of this dimension of childhood experience. A similar gender experience may be at work to explain the fact that 74 per cent of males recalled being allowed to talk at meal times as a child, but only 60 per cent of females recalled that freedom. What cannot be denied is that structuring the data not only reveals differences raised by more intuitive and qualitative analyses, but that it offers a distinct contribution to those intuitive qualitative insights and to the theoretical debates of which they are part.[7]

One of the most important aspects of aggregating oral history interviews is that it reflects a decision to *take account of all the evidence available, even those cases which are contrary to one's thesis.* I have found this a valuable discipline even in analysing a few interviews. The danger of working from selected extracts is that it is the most striking interviews which command attention, and the feeling that one knows the material well enough to generalize without coding and structuring the data can be dangerously misleading. It is this approach which will ultimately decide whether oral evidence remains essentially illustrative or whether it can be used to form better historical generalizations. One really should not need to belabour the case for these simple procedures to be applied to oral evidence; it is enough to reverse the question and ask what sort of historical interpretation are we presented with without them. The answer is quite negative. One result is conventional history simply illustrated with the odd extract chosen mainly for its dramatic impact or publishable attractions; the main interpretative framework, however, has come from other sources and the oral evidence is simply a piece of dramatic colour. Another approach is to publish the interviews as directly as possible thus reducing history to personal retrospective testimony; but the extracts all have to be selected and edited and are inevitably shaped by the compiler's conscious or unconscious purposes. There is no means of knowing whether they are representative of those interviewed, much less whether they are in any sense typical of wider categories such as class. And even where an author has made very careful use of oral evidence through careful evaluation and fair selection, there would still be a great advantage in being able to triangulate such use with the synoptic whole which is possible through simple statistical procedures.

10   Patterned responses

> Moreover the studies make use of very diverse theoretical
> frameworks: symbolic interactionism of course, but also Sartrian
> Marxism, structuralist Marxism, cultural anthropology, historical
> social psychology, psycho-history, role theory, interpretative sociology
> – to name but a few.
>
> Daniel Bertaux (ed.)
> *Biography and Society* (Sage 1981), p. 6

So far the process of collecting and analysing interviews has been
presented largely within a positivistic framework of knowledge.
While I am critical of many aspects of the process as applied to oral
history, it has been urged as the most effective methodology for
collecting the information, assessing its typicality and establishing
the distribution of social phenomena. It is, however, limited in
scope and incomplete in itself. Some would argue that utilizing such
a framework for the initial procedures prevents the use of alternative approaches to interpreting the evidence. I disagree. I am convinced of the value of positivistic methodology as argued so far,
while rejecting positivistic philosophical assumptions about indi-
vidualism and society. There is a dialectical relationship with individuals forming society and society forming individuals, and
alternative approaches to historical and social knowledge from
interviews are validly based on the perception of people as creators
and bearers of economic and social relationships. Each individual
oral history, therefore, is an exemplar and reveals the history of the
period through the relationships of the individual with others, lived
within the constraints of the economic and social. In theory, therefore, even one interview can reveal the relationships experienced by
those sharing similar time, spatial and social locations. The pattern
of one life will, apart from personal contingencies, follow the same
essential trajectory of others in that economic and social position.

   This approach is overtly distanced from the traditional use of
biographical material. Bertaux argues that biography is a bourgeois

concept which focuses on individuals and interprets life mainly in terms of the self-will and psychological drives of the 'hero'.[1] So although this approach takes the individual life as a unique and unified source of information it is actually arguing that the individual is not the focus of interpretation. The point is that people live their lives within the material and cultural boundaries of their time span, and so life histories are exceptionally effective historical sources because through the totality of lived experience they reveal *relations* between individuals and social forces which are rarely apparent in other sources. Above all, the information is historical and dynamic in that it reveals changes of experience through time, as opposed to the static analysis of social surveys and statistical correlations.

It has been frequently and justifiably argued that oral history is particularly suited for uncovering 'real' relationships whether in the home or at work. Individuals are moulded and shaped by their immediate experiences; the wider social and economic forces are mediated through the familial and the local.[2] In a radical article Ferrarotti argues that as the primary social group shapes life history it is the social formation upon which life stories shed most light, and as it is the social formation most immediately responsible for the individual's experience of the wider social and historical forces it is this ensemble of relationships which might prove the most fruitful focus of study: 'For the individual biography, why not substitute the biography of the primary group, as the basic heuristic unit of a renewed biographical method?' He goes on to argue that this would avoid the dangers of sliding '. . . into nominalism, into an atomistic logic and into social psychology' which is always present in a biographical method. He goes on to assert that:

> The individual is not the founder of the social, but rather its sophisticated product. Paradoxically, the true elementary unit of the social is, in our opinion, the primary group: an apparent complex system which constitutes, in reality, the most simple object under sociological observation.[3]

He acknowledges that there are difficulties in establishing how one might define what constitutes the biography of a group, but certainly it is a perspective which maintains a materialistic emphasis on economic and social forces as the focus of social analysis and historical change rather than the individual. In his view Sartre's definition of the individual as a 'singular universal' should be utilized and developed. Certainly this approach would avoid the ever present danger that life histories can tend to trivialize and depoliticize social history.

This approach to analysis through the individual as an exemplar of social relationships, or through the primary relations of an individual, is not, however, necessarily exclusive to any one philosophical position, but is a classical sociological assumption:

> Society is not a simple aggregate of individuals; the system formed by their association represents a specific reality possessing its own characteristics . . . If, then, we begin with the individual, we shall be able to understand nothing of what takes place in the group. In a word, there is between psychology and sociology the same break in continuity as between biology and physiochemical sciences. Consequently, whenever a social phenomenon is directly explained by a psychological phenomenon one can be sure than the explanation is invalid.[4]

The crucial point is to avoid allowing psychological explanations to be used where social and historical ones are more appropriate. Fundamental to the historical analysis of individual life histories are the similarities apparent in the lives of individuals who have experienced the same set of structural relations. These will be most apparent where the opportunities and alternatives were most limited. For example, a turn of the century pit village, or small mill town; where – having established the pattern of life from school to work, through courtship to parenthood – the lives, work, income, leisure, culture and so forth of one informant would differ from others in only unimportant details from life to death. It is doubtful whether conducting a hundred interviews in a random sample from such a village would reveal anything really more significant than a dozen or so chosen haphazardly. The need for large statistical analysis is unnecessary because the pattern of life and the correlation between areas of experience are part of lived experience visible in the trajectory and activities of people's lives.

The force of this approach became apparent to me through my research into East Anglian fishermen where, for example, although all fishermen had the reputation of being very superstitious, it became obvious in fewer than a dozen interviews that there were very different levels of belief within different sectors of the fishing industry, and the content of the informants' accounts implied that it was practised according to crew status. In addition, because superstition was located within the person's life history, the reasons why some sectors were more superstitious than others were quite implicit in the accounts of the material conditions of their economic and industrial experience. In other words, the content of a few interviews revealed that the category 'fishermen' was too large and that more appropriate categories of 'trawlermen' and 'driftermen' were needed to group the reported experiences. Although I am sure that most oral historians must have experienced similar insights from comparatively few interviews, the most direct claim that a full understanding of economic and social structures can be had from a limited number of interviews comes from Bertaux:

> The first life story taught us a great deal; so did the second and the third. By the fifteenth we had begun to understand the pattern of sociostructural relations which makes up the life of a bakery worker. By the twenty-fifth, adding the knowledge we had from life stories and bakers, we knew we had it; a clear picture of this structural pattern and of its recent transformations. New life stories confirmed what we had understood, adding slight individual variations. We stopped at thirty: there was no point going further. We knew already what we wanted to know.[5]

There is a reality principle which can scarcely be denied in asserting the strength of this method of interpretation. It clearly is informative and humanistic and it is the sort of analysis which historians have always applied to personal documents. Nevertheless, there are methodological problems with this approach. Gagnon criticizes it because, in accepting direct testimony as 'speaking for itself' it becomes a form of positivism and open to the criticism applicable to that methodology. She argues that applying this sort of typographical logic to life stories does not avoid the problems associated with coding and measurement because one is using 'a nominal level complex measurement'.[6] This may be rather synonymous with 'commonsense', but whatever measure one is using (and I think that Gagnon's point has some force) there is no doubt that the strength of having the account of the various dimensions of life together in one lived experience gives all the data a particular strength lacking in virtually any other source of evidence; and certainly lacking in any other widespread documentary form.

This method of constructing historical interpretations from a limited number of interviews has much in common with how historians, sociologists and social anthropologists have often studied local communities. A major advantage of the oral history approach is that one does not collect just biographical 'facts' pertaining to the informants – their occupation, address, social class, politics and so on. One collects also their memories of what they saw and knew of the environment in which they lived – that one street was 'rough' and another 'posh'. That a newly-built street in Lowestoft, Suffolk, became known as 'Skippers' Row' is a comment on the prosperity of the drifting industry and the high earnings of successful skippers just before the First World War. This information about the industry does not have to come from fishermen: it can come from anyone who knew the area well. Where an arbitrary number of interviews includes a variety of occupations, social classes, gender, chapel and church goers, drinkers and teetotallers, large and small families, and various physical locations within the community, there comes a point where it is unlikely that any significant experience has not been included if only indirectly. This simply expresses a point made earlier that research carried out by local history groups or individuals will often have its own logic of inquiry and the authenticity which comes from that (although it could be argued that, through taking a variety of experiences in one community, one has effectively 'sampled' the local population, and has implemented the strength of that methodology). In any case, treating each interview as a unique source of social information is a good procedure if only because it emphasizes the value of each informant as a complete and unique case to be interviewed as fully as anyone else, and where these are taken from one occupation the experiences overlap in time and space so the interviews validate one another.

This is a sound historical method, but it is slightly different from the more focused method used by Bertaux about which there are at least two reservations to be made. First, it leads to research which is limited to the researcher's own immediate purposes and not to the fuller account that an informant might give, and so limits the potential each informant could make to the historical record and future research. Second, it accepts as given that oral evidence can never be sufficiently available to permit analysis at the morphological level.

The first point becomes apparent where Bertaux describes how, as research into a single occupation progresses, much of the information given by each informant becomes repetitious as everyone's descriptions of work experience goes over much the same ground. He argues that once the stage has been reached where the researchers fully understand the work process, those questions can be dropped in order to concentrate on other areas of ideologies and relations which need to be explored in more depth. Bertaux undoubtedly respects his informants and perceives this dropping of routine questions as giving them a more constructive role in the research. But the danger of following a single-minded piece of research to 'saturation point' is that it creates a situation where informants are treated less as integral wholes and more as sources who simply extend or complete the knowledge that the researcher has achieved at the time the interview takes place. It also loses the advantages that an interview ranging across the full experience of the informant could have; when interviews are partial and focused on solving the present problems of the researchers they become bricks in that single edifice rather than informative life histories in their own right, and of wider use to future historians. An associated defect of this researcher-centred model of interviewing is that it loses the advantages which detailed probing of material circum- stances give in stimulating the memory and helping to ensure that the 'ideologies' expressed are in period. By not reimmersing infor- mants in the detail of the past one is tapping memory at a more superficial level than would otherwise be the case.

In spite of the valuable insights which come from this method it is limited simply because it is so self-enclosed. It seeks just a sufficient number of accounts from those directly involved in a situation; and yet in some areas no amount of such focused interviewing will provide a full or rounded source. For example, a conference report on women's history and oral history held in France in 1981 gives the following account of the proceedings:

> Danielle Tucat explained how midwives would talk freely about every detail of their work – except the advice they gave on abortion and contraception. This role was against the ethic of their profession, and none would admit to their own part in it; only that of others. Yet as Françoise Cribier insisted, it was a very important role which many women who had received such advice certainly remembered.[7]

This is a salutary reminder that sometimes those with the most inside and direct knowledge of events feel the most need to conceal the reality. Now this is not proof of the 'falsity' of oral evidence but a simple example of the need to consider very carefully where, how and from whom particular types of information will be gained. The very strength of this method of examining a number of interviews from the same occupation and reaching 'saturation point' is also its weakness. Those informants are not only the bearers of the material forces which shaped them but also the bearers of the cultural and ideological ones which limit what they are prepared to reveal of that experience. The advantage of the wider sampling approach is precisely that it collects information from those who were outside an experience as well as from those who were within it, and more crucially from those who were at the other pole of a relationship. I doubt whether one will ever fully understand what doctors do unless some of their patients are also interviewed.

Those objections are linked to my second reservation about this approach – that it fails to acknowledge the potential of oral evidence as a more general source. Bertaux argues that they avoided the necessity of a conventionally understood representative sample because:

> . . . we went through a process of *saturation of knowledge*. This process confers to the idea of 'representivity' a completely different meaning. In short, we may say that our sample is representative, not at the morphological level (at the level of superficial description), but at the sociological level, at the level of sociostructural relations.[8]

If my reservations about dropping questions and the effect of this on the quality of recall and the value of the interviews for future research are put to one side, there is no doubt that at the practical level of historical and social analysis his research method is extremely effective for some projects. He makes the distinction between the value of the morphological and the sociostructural:

> These two levels should not be confused. If for instance, one wants to know how a given population is going to vote in the next election, the first level is the right one. But if one wants to understand how the practice of voting and choosing for whom to vote takes place, then it is the second level which is relevant.[9]

This is noncontentious, but what I do not yet accept as proven is the implication that oral history cannot contribute to a morphological analysis of the past. As it is accepted that survey methodology contributes to knowledge of political distributions today there is no fundamental reason why oral history archives could not be used to provide such an analysis for the past. So many aspects of social behaviour are not understood – from who socialized children or how, to ways and means of controlling the workplace. Sociostructural analysis might provide the understanding of the relations involved, but that still leaves unknown the distribution of phenomena among different occupations, regions and classes. But this knowledge would be a large gain simply because the size and distribution of a phenomenon as well as its dynamics are essential facets of historical understanding. With the growing number of interviews available in archives it should be possible to come to some conclusions about distributions even if they do lack formal statistical validity.

*Part Four   Memory, Theory and
Purpose*

11 Memory

> In recent years the study of memory has grown enormously. Each year sees several hundred new articles reporting research on remembering . . . It will be evident from this . . . that despite a vast amount of empirical evidence, the encapsulation of the memory phenomena within a coherent theoretical framework is as elusive as ever.
>
> M. M. Gruneberg and P. Morris (eds.)
> *Aspects of Memory* (Methuen 1978)

The three preceding parts of the book have dealt with oral history largely on the basis of the practical process by which oral historians conduct their research and how each step of that practice affects the final value and authenticity of the evidence collected. We now turn to an overt consideration of how that practice relates to more theoretical and political issues. These are presented separately as chapters on memory, theory, and purpose; but as the position held on one of those issues largely determines what can reasonably be held on the others, the argument requires the entire section to be considered as a whole. As the ultimate authenticity of retrospective evidence depends upon the degree to which memory is a reliable repository of past experience this must be the first consideration. One's model of how memory works is a crucial determinant of possible theoretical evaluations of the value and purpose of retrospective oral evidence.

Models of how the memory works, physically or psychologically, appear to be still at the stage of speculation. The studies of memory conducted by psychologists have thrown very little scientific light on what, why or how people's minds select some impressions of daily life to remember.[1] In terms of establishing the authenticity of oral evidence the careful historical evaluation of the information itself is probably as sound a procedure as anything which can be offered by psychologists. In spite of this, or perhaps because of it, some historians maintain an ingrained suspicion of the authenticity of long-term memory. This is most clearly expressed as an unargued assumption that memory simply fades with time. At the level of introspection, of practical experience and of psychiatric work this model of memory is clearly incorrect. Informants who have forgotten that you are coming to see them, and who cannot remember events over the last few years, can frequently give clear and detailed accounts of their early life. And here, it is worth distinguishing 'memory' from 'emotional intensity' because there is psychoanalytical evidence of the suppression of certain intensely experienced emotions. One may have very clear memories of a particular event because it was a moment of high emotion (a bereavement for example) and be able to recall the situation and sequence of events accurately but without the same degree of emotion. The degree to which this affects the quality of the memory as historical evidence depends upon what one wishes to establish from the evidence. If, to continue with the example, one wants to know about the rituals associated with death – who came to the funeral, what clothes were worn and so on – this loss of emotional intensity would scarcely affect the authenticity of the evidence. If, however, one is trying to record lived experience at the level of feeling, then clearly this loss seriously weakens the value of the evidence. This can affect many dimensions of evidence: the passion of political commitment or of religious conviction is really part of the historical experience and some of the reality of activities is lost if the original emotional intensity cannot be recalled. It must be accepted that we never have direct access to memory. Even were the informant capable of recalling emotive content, it has to be communicated and few people have the verbal skills (even where they have the desire) to relate past emotional states. This aspect of loss is more serious to those historians who believe that oral history can give them some *direct access to experience* of the past than to those who accept that they collect mainly the *remembered aspects of activity* in the past.

To claim that all memory simply and inevitably fades would entail the end of oral history as a worthwhile historical enterprise: the recording of current affairs would remain the only feasible activity. It is a position that has been advanced:

> We have drawn up a ten-point questionnaire, which a sympathetic interviewer could put to the leaders of an institution at regular intervals – say, every twelve months. . . . The records would then also serve as a valuable resource for future historians, their contemporary nature helping to ensure a high degree of factual accuracy in recording the unfolding of policy and thinking. Indeed, because of their doubts

about the distortions of longer-term memory, some critics would regard such contemporary and regular recording of information as the
only valid role of oral history.[2]

While it is only prudent to examine the potential fallibility of longer-
term memories the above quotation goes to the opposite extreme by
according contemporary statements an amazing degree of over-
credulity, particularly those given by contemporary elites.[3] For it is
precisely this type of contemporary documentation which runs the
highest risk of being false and biased because those involved feel
obliged to defend and justify their current actions. The questionnaire cited consists mainly of questions which evaluate the success
with which the elite persons have fulfilled their tasks over the
previous year. It is not very realistic to expect factual evidence
about the relative success with which they have done their jobs to
come from the very people whose well-rewarded survival relies on
their maintaining a successful image. They are most unlikely to
reveal policy misjudgements or the personal advantages which
affected decision making. Few 'elites' would acknowledge the
secret developments, the failures and mistakes which their organizations want concealed. To imagine for one moment that because
the 'truth' is fresh in their minds it will be put into words and
recorded for all time is to show a touching faith in the capacity for
public self-criticism which has never been conspicuous amongst the
great and the good, and even less in evidence amongst the rich and
ruthless. Such an approach to authenticity could probably succeed
only with some artistic elites where their contemporary creative
activity is what they would most want to project. But unless the
informant has an absolute advantage in disclosing the truth (or a
rare commitment to it) then contemporary recording will reveal
only the degree of dissimulation being practised at that particular
time. One might note in passing that it is just such contemporary
evidence, distorted by current pressures, which becomes the historical documents against which the authenticity of retrospective
evidence is then held in question. I doubt whether one could gain an
insight into the true story of any major business or government
department from its principals before they had retired. Even then it
would be unlikely, short of their experiencing political radicalization
or defecting somewhere. The point is that the further away one is
from the self-interest and advantages to be gained in giving a particular account of an event, and the nearer one approaches a death-
bed confession, the more likely it is that an authentic account will

emerge: on the whole, time and distance from a situation weaken the pressures to dissemble.

At all events, one can put aside the simplistic view that the degree of authenticity of oral evidence has any relationship to contemporaneity. If it had we would be obliged to accept the 'truth' of contemporary statements from the Kim Philby's of this world and not their retrospective accounts of their actual activities given from long-term memory after the events. The past will be recalled with greatest fidelity when there is a commitment to accuracy, and that can have more effect on authenticity than the structure of memory itself. My own view is that many elites are always so subject to contemporary pressures, as well as being conscious of the longer scrutiny of history, that nothing they say could ever be taken at face value.

The experience of three research projects in Germany came very close to the same conclusion. In attempting to document recent 'political labour history' through interviews they came to the conclusion that oral evidence was unreliable. This was because informants had been active in German labour organizations as communists, or in other left-wing groups, and had passed through nazism, de-nazification, social democracy, the Cold War and had experienced so many political and organizational twists and turns that a number of them now simply lied about their past. Others could not remember with any clarity the specific events that concerned the researchers. Clearly the recent political history of a country can intensify the effectiveness with which oral history can be expected to record the truth of events, especially through elite interviewing on politically sensitive topics. In spite of the difficulties the researchers had interviewing political activists, their general experience led them to conclude that 'memory' is, in fact, essentially reliable and accurate for other types of historical information:

> The conditions of everyday life are firmly held in the memory and hardly distorted at all by later experiences or changes in attitude. Maybe this is the only field where oral history can be regarded as a direct way of tapping the past, although it still requires an interviewer who can open up informants' minds to those areas that they may otherwise take for granted and neglect.[4]

Certainly their experience, and the experience of others dealing with elites or other sensitive groups, gives no warrant for those critics of 'empirical' oral history who argue that memories of the past must be remembered *through* subsequent events.[5] In this model memory is assumed to be a non-historical entity with only current interpretations of previous experience; not so much a memory as a constantly up-dated file of information in which old data is constantly modified, altered and changed by new experience. No reference back to 'pure' impressions is possible. That this theoretical position shows no contact with the memories of real people will be apparent to any individual capable of introspection or of listening to others: the usual complaint is that grandparents and parents relate precisely the same stories over and over again. My memory, for example, is full of 'facts' – hours of work, wages, places visited, leisure activity, length of working week and holidays – which have not changed since the event. And this is the case also for non-material facts. I am aware that I have changed my cultural, social and political values as I have lived longer and enjoyed a changing experience and contact with new ideas and ideologies: occasionally I can even remember the 'when' and 'why' it happened. The crucial point is that I am aware that my interpretation, attitudes and values have changed and that what I would have had to relate about my past had I been interviewed at different points in time would have been evaluated differently; but at each point of time I would have (properly interviewed) related a similar factual account including those previous states of mind. They are not recalled and homogenized *through* present consciousness; the memory of different experiences and values is, indeed, *part* of my present consciousness. Experience convinces me that most other people experience memory in a similar way. That life and memories are sequential gives no warrant for assuming that the brain parallels this structure and stores memory traces sequentially, with newer memories lying atop earlier memories: it may place them to their side or even under them. The way in which many elderly people retain clear memories of their early years while forgetting the recent and immediate past demonstrates the strength of early memories; and if the recent past cannot be recalled while the distant past can then there are some grounds for assuming that these early memories are directly accessed.

It should also be acknowledged that the ability to recall the past is not a consistent ability. Psychologists have identified a period when elderly people appear unusually willing and able to recall their past, and perhaps the exceptional quality of some interviews comes from actually meeting an informant during that period. But memories can suddenly flood back with a vividness not previously experienced for no apparent reason at any age. The author of a recent autobiography has recounted how her memory functioned:

> [she] could hardly remember anything about her childhood until four years ago, when one day walking along a Spanish beach, she suddenly heard in her mind the clearest conversation between her now dead parents . . . [she states] 'within 48 hours all of my childhood came back to me' . . . [she] spent the next two weeks writing down her memories as they streamed out.[6]

This spontaneous type of memory which almost forces the person to record it is unusual: most recall needs prompting, although the mere fact of another person showing an interest can stimulate hitherto unrecalled memories. I believe my informants when some of them announce, usually on our second meeting, that since talking about the past with me they have recalled episodes in their life that they are not conscious of having previously recalled since the event. I believe that some people, at least, experience 'pure' recall without the distortion of contemporary rationalization. But remembering is not the same as relating.

Any discussion on the functioning of memory needs to distinguish what people are willing to relate from what they remember. For example, a number of elderly women talking about their early married life volunteered the information that they were pregnant when they were married; had they been interviewed some thirty or more years earlier such disclosures would have been most unlikely. By contrast, I suspect that any racist opinions and activities would be more difficult to elicit now than they would have been in the past. But this is neither a weakness of memory nor a problem for oral history. One positive advantage of retrospective interviewing is that the 'dominant ideology' has changed and what could not be said then can be said now. Naturally enough the obverse of that advantage is that what informants will be willing to relate (as distinct from being able to remember) will be censored by present cultural and social pressures. But even the subjects which are taboo now can be more easily approached through 'distancing' the subject as being accepted behaviour of a previous age and not now part of the informant's values or practices. In other words the advantages and disadvantages of retrospective oral evidence will be more likely affected by social constraints than by failures of memory. The essential point is to be aware that memory and social context interact in complex ways which require careful evaluation in each particular case.

The term 'popular memory' is frequently encountered in discussions on oral history, but as often happens to a term lacking an agreed definition it has come to be used in two quite different ways. Originally it appeared as a shorthand term for oral history taken from ordinary people, carrying with it the assumption that this was a more democratic and radical source of history than that produced from the records generated by the state, major organizations and the media. It is linked to the notion of people speaking for themselves and the access to a direct and authentic source of history stemming from the remembered experience of working people. More recently it appears to denote a generalized collective image of the past which, although held by the people, does not come from them. In this view 'popular memory' is heavily influenced and shaped by the institutions with economic, political and social power. It emphasizes the undoubted role of the media and institutions such as the monarchy, military parades and tattoos, or the National Trust in popularizing certain images of the past at the expense of others. It argues that memory cannot simply be a memory of life as it was, but that anyone's memory must be selectively distorted by the class power behind the projection of these images. In other words 'memory' is constructed from past and present ideology and is not a recalled impression of 'things as they were'. In its more extreme formulation it virtually denies memory the capacity to preserve distinct states of mind, and perceives it as a part of an ever-changing present consciousness. This perspective rejects our common ability to distinguish past and present, and, if accepted, the argument for doing oral history as a study of the 'past' would virtually disappear. If the remembered 'past' is a construct of present ideology and power then clearly it really is the preserve of contemporary studies not historians. If oral historians are bound to reject this position they should acknowledge that memory is formed within the structures of economic and cultural power and the degree to which this affects individual memories deserves careful consideration. To establish the way in which memories are shaped, recalled, forgotten and interpreted is an essential task which, as yet, oral historians have not seriously tackled. Given their own failure to address the subject they should welcome the interest shown by those studying contemporary culture.

At the moment, however, the notion of popular memory seems

to be rather reified and lacking in any firm material location. The importance of how history is presented in national life for shaping general perception of the past may be almost self-evident; but to use the concept of 'popular memory' to enhance the authenticity of oral evidence would entail much careful research. Even if one puts aside, for the moment, how the dominant memory articulates with the different national traditions within Britain; people from different regions, occupations or cultural backgrounds have varying degrees of exposure to the dominant national popular memory and media. Local manifestations do not always reinforce the national image – a notable example being miners' galas – and there are, at one level, a multiplicity of popular memories differing from region to region, town to town and even village to village according to the economic, political and social history of the location. The actualities of life in the inter-war period will interact rather differently with a dominant media image according to whether one lived along the Thames or the Tyne. It is precisely through careful interviewing that one might gain some impression of the variety of economic and social experience and how this constructed differing attitudes and values. Individuals have differing real experiences and different memories with which 'national' memory will have greater or lesser congruence: dominant ideology is never simply passively accepted, it is reacted to according to the real experience of those who receive it. 'Ideology' itself, dominant or otherwise, is also a historical and changing phenomenon held differentially by different groups at different times and it dominates some people more than others. Elites (including academics) are more prone to rationalize and revise their memories in light of their present ideology than are most people whose direct life experiences are less easily forgotten or changed.

The whole subject of historical memory is one which needs further theoretical and empirical investigation, but my experience of interviewing leads me to suspect that *individual* memories are rather less malleable than some supporters of the dominant ideology perspective would have us believe. The Popular Memory Group seem to come close to denying a person's ability to recall their own past in oral accounts and cite Koss's observation that servants, used as informants, may have seen popular media presentations of their work history and been influenced by them. Well, they may of been, but to assume that working people are so plastic as to have years of real experience transmuted by a few hours of secondhand and false imagery is to exhibit a rather odd view of the mental integrity of ordinary people. My experience of interviewing is that the recall of working experience is somewhat more durable than that. When someone recounts the routine of a day's work it is not one specific day, but the pattern of innumerable days in that particular period, the imprint of which can often still be seen in calluses on the skin and the very posture of the person. Television may produce idyllic programmes about rural life but anyone who laboured in the fields knows it was hard and low-paid. I would agree that it is very easy to collect a few 'false' generalizations by ill-prepared and poor interviewing. A superficial few minutes for a media presentation will be most likely to collect just those generalizations, derived from popular memory, which we have found are later contradicted by the authenticity of detailed recall. Any interview showing a serious historical interest in the informant's personal experiences will soon progress beyond such surface accounts to something more authentic. What appears to convince many historians that interviewees must be reporting some form of 'false consciousness' is the fact that the majority of people rarely express resentment, bitterness or political radicalism after a lifetime of being exploited. But manual labour has its satisfactions which exist whether the activity is properly rewarded or not, and it should be no surprise that many people who worked far too hard, and too long, communicate pride in their work and their endurance. It is not proof of the power of the 'dominant ideology' when informants relate satisfactions stemming from the process of production experienced within unsatisfactory relations of production: what is false and romantic is when the interviewer collects only the generalized sense of satisfaction and leaves the detail of the material conditions to silence.

Glen Elder has emphasized the importance of cohort experience in history and its effect on the formation of memory 'generations' – that is to say people who share a social experience which is historically distinct from others. This type of analysis might provide a method of charting the course of popular memory, how it is formed and how it relates to individual recall. A person's birth year places them in an historical context and stratifies their experiences: whether their schooling was before or after an educational reform, an expansion in university education or its contraction, whether they entered the job market in a time of boom or bust will very much determine their individual experiences and their social perspectives.

People are not only stratified by class or separated by gender but are also segmented within those categories by cohort experience: they leave school, get married, have children and so on at different points in history. Cohort analysis emphasizes the importance of historical changes in shaping the experience of people rather than the personality or enterprise of the individual. Elder cites Davis as identifying 'nostalgia as the core process by which generations are born'.[7] He defines nostalgia as meaning the collective distillation of scenes, events and practices which were experienced but which are now lost (for example, the shared experience of those with memories of the 1920s and 1930s – for many of the working class the experience/memories of poverty, unemployment and the Means Test; compared with the post-war generation's experience/ memories of the 1950s and 1960s with Social Welfare, virtually full employment, the extension of paid holidays and so forth; now being followed by the creation of another cohort of unemployed and so on). This process of generating cohort memories is most noticeable and distinctive in times of abrupt change, and oral evidence should be able to chart the complexities and boundaries of these experiences and relate them to the way in which different sectors of the population in different situations remember the social, industrial and political situation.

I would argue that unless the images of recent history reflect something of the reality of personal experience individuals will reject it as unsound. But this brings the issue back to what is 'popular memory' and, more importantly, what are its implications for oral history. It must be agreed that the dominant ideology and media presentations do affect people's historical 'knowledge'. For example, anyone who did not have experience of domestic service may have their historical image of it shaped by media presentations and so accept as part of their historical knowledge the image of life below stairs as it is shown on television. In this the theory is correct: the dominant ideology shapes 'popular memory'. But if one were researching an oral history of domestic service one would not interview those people who were neither domestic servants nor their employers. The individual oral history accounts from the memories of those who actually lived that experience are very different from 'popular' presentations. And this is so whether the popular image overstates the pleasures or pains of that experience. So although the 'popular memory' gained from dominant institutions may hold a false impression, this does not preclude the collection of accurate accounts from those whose personal experience gives them the authority to reject it. Oral historians do not interview a generalized and abstract 'popular memory' held by the masses, they interview people, individuals with personal memories of specific social and historical locations. Popular memory can be acknowledged false without casting the least shadow on the authenticity of oral history properly practised.

What is not remembered (said) is more of a problem than what is remembered (said). Louisa Passerini introduced the notion of 'silences' from her research on the Italian working class.[8] She found that there were gaps in their personal accounts for the years under fascism and what she calls 'inconsistent' answers, which are accounts which make no reference to major historical events and processes. These silences and inconsistencies are explained as a collective self-censorship, a 'political scar', left by fascism. The idea of a collective silence is supported by oral history research on the nazi period in Germany. That participants might avoid talking about the fascist period in European countries where those regimes took power is a reasonable hypothesis. Its more general significance is the implication that if a whole cohort of informants avoid particular subjects then this factor is bound to be at work in less dramatically obvious periods and places with the risk of systematic distortion by collective omission. At the very least it is a reminder that no historical source is complete and each source needs to be scrutinized for its defects. Such 'silences' are not evidence of the fallibility of oral evidence but indicate the effect on testimony of changes in political and social culture and the subjectivity of the narrator. Passerini's method was to allow the informants to be largely self-directing at the beginning of an interview and this is where the silences were found. As the interviewer questioned more deeply on various aspects of life under fascism such silences were either filled-in or left as known areas of no, or limited, information. It is not appropriate to pursue her work in detail here, but I was struck by the realization that a number of my informants followed a similar pattern of 'silence' in so far as a similar age-cohort would account for their early life, their entry to the workforce, their First World War experiences, settling down afterwards and then largely ignore the inter-war period (a silence) to take up their story of events with the Second World War. This is a similar structure to Passerini's interviews. She quotes one informant talking about the violent clashes with the fascists, where one sentence runs: '. . . in any case we went on like this. Then the bombing started, . . .', thus jumping from 1925 when the political clashes in that factory ended with the victory of the fascists, to the air raids of the 1940s in the Second World War. Passerini perceives this as censoring the fascist period.

Given the history of fascism 'silences' may well be a factor in Italian oral history. But my own observations on the way in which people narrate their experiences leads me to wonder whether it is due to the way in which they (European/Western) measure and remember time. Informants do dismiss long timespans with a casual 'Oh, well things just carried on until we moved' or 'And then the war started' or a similar *event* punctuated their existing circumstances. People relate their life histories in terms of 'change', particularly where informants are narrating freely, when 'What happened next?' seems to dominate over the detailed exposition of a long period of little variation. I suspect that this is due less to ideological dimensions than to the conventions of story-telling and the routine of daily life. It could explain the interview I have already cited where the informant gave more time and detail to relating some short-term employments than to his fifty years with one firm. The events which serve as punctuation points to memory are either aspects of national history which cause personal change, such as conscription, war work, air raids and so forth; or they are personal events such as births, deaths, marriage, occupational or geographical mobility: in other words a *change* of circumstances. An editorial of *History Workshop* (in a comment on Passerini's article) makes the point that British oral history finds very little about the General Strike and speculates as to whether the same self-censorship is at work. This is perhaps not a useful comparison as fascism lasted for years and the General Strike for only days. But how people remember their history is a profound issue which can probably be answered only by comparative studies in different countries, where by interviewing groups of the same birth cohort who spent their lives under the different political development of their own country one could compare the accounts to examine how people periodize their lives and to what they give most salience.

What is clear is that memory is not just a biological structure which could, properly interrogated, reproduce an accurate mirror image of the past. Even if it could, there is every reason to doubt that the majority of people would be either willing or able to describe their experience in full. But if most memories are prone to simplification and elision this does not make them any less authentic an image than a sketch of a landscape: each may have simplified, compressed and abstracted, yet each can convey a recognizably true aspect of the reality. It is not only a matter of individual psychology that some will delineate or elide different details of the reality; gender, as well as class, affects which aspects of life people remember as well as how they relate it. Isabelle Bertaux-Wiame has argued that women are better than men at recalling family matters such as how many kin they had, when they died, what occuaptions they had, where they moved to and similar details of the social network.[9] I am sure that this is also true of interviews in this country. She explains this as the result of men holding a view of themselves as self-willed individuals who relate their lives mainly in terms of their occupational and personal experience, whereas women, because they are tied more often to the domestic sphere and rely on recip-rocal relationships with kin, often relate their life history through the use of 'we' rather than 'I' which gives a much fuller picture of the web of social relations and networks which influence so many events. But given the traditional role divisions this is not surprising; women cared for the previous generation and they reared the next, work made more effective within a family network. But whatever the cause of these differences, the realization that testimonies are bound to be shaped by gender and class experiences in how, and what, is narrated is a valuable one. Bertaux-Wiame has also applied this type of analysis to the accounts from within one gender em-ployed in the same occupation. The accounts from male bakers gave systematically different explanations for the hardships they en-dured during their early years in the trade as apprentices according to whether they had since become master bakers themselves or remained as waged employees. This is used as an example of how subsequent experience and present position affects the way in which people remember and relate their earlier experiences. Although if her point has any logic to it (and it has), it is not clear why she should then assert that it is the masters who have 'reconstructed the mean-ing of the facts'; if the present distorts the past the effect cannot be restricted to the employers alone, the workmen's testimonies must also have been reconstructed by their present. But her account is interesting because although she recognizes the effect of the present on the evaluative aspects of the past, she states that the 'empirical' account of the work routine is the same in both cases. The import-ant point is to be aware of the distinction between referential information about the past and the evaluations of it. Bertaux-Wiame's perspective adds considerable credence to the view that there is a solid base of factual information in oral testimonies which remains constant whatever the subsequent experience of the informant. This is encouraging for those who want to use oral evidence for an account of the past. It fits with my fieldwork experience and intro-spection: my informants are convinced that they have accurate memories of some events, and I am aware that my memory of some events has remained constant although my evaluation of them has changed. The process of interviewing with an emphasis on activity and material surroundings of the past should increase the auth-enticity of the referential content and decrease the contemporary evaluative content.

Memory is a complex phenomenon which cannot be tested for truth by the application of a set of rules or by the technology of a brainscan. Memory is a form of historical evidence which, like any other type of historical evidence, needs to be evaluated as such. The starting point for this evaluation must be the degree to which the memories are set into a context of time and place. For example, a person who states their own wage at a certain point in time may be correct, and if this statement is fixed to a specific time 'event' such as the end of an apprenticeship, the beginning of married life or a public event then the likelihood of accuracy for that point is high. It is even higher if the memory contains comparisons drawn from that date; for example, an accurate statement of the wage levels in other occupations will confirm that the informant has an accurate recall of aspects beyond direct personal experience. Where there is no spe-cific event to serve as a point at which to place the informant's memory of one aspect – for example, memory of a wage-rate only as 'between the wars' or other long period – the memory might be more accurately located when placed within the context of place of residence, the number of children in the family by then, or even which clothes or songs were the current fashion. In other words a myriad of contextual details could date an 'inter-war' memory more precisely to a particular year. These factual statements can be triangulated with documentary evidence (or other oral testimony), and where informants' memories have not only tied their personal experience to a specific time, but have also accurately placed it within the recalled material context of social factors, then there are pragmatic grounds for accepting their memories as good historical evidence. If what they have to add about those aspects of historical inquiry were not recorded in contemporary sources, or were recorded from biased sources, then there is some reason for assuming that such memories will have the substance as well as the time and context of those aspects authentically placed.

12 Theory

A much more implicit orientation arises when the researcher claims *not* to probe, guide or ask questions but simply wants the subject to talk spontaneously and freely, revealing the flux and contradictions of everyday subjective reality. Yet this, of course, is itself a theoretical orientation (closely allied to symbolic interactionism) and will encourage ambiguities and contradictions to be found.

Ken Plummer
Documents of Life (George Allen & Unwin 1983), p.123

Plummer makes the point that theory is inescapable because it is 'an orientation to research': as such every piece of oral history research is conducted within the framework of implicit theoretical assumptions. My aim has been to discuss oral history as a practical activity and to consider ways of improving the authenticity of oral evidence, and many people would consider the implicit 'theoretical orientation' excessively positivistic. The practice, however, is not tied to one epistemology; sampling and questionnaires are part of a positivistic framework, but by then using an open-ended interview one steps into symbolic interactionism, as cited by Plummer above. There is also the matter of the use of the evidence as well as its generation. Historians learn to utilize whatever evidence survives in the records without being able to control, or even know, the theoretical framework of its generation. In any case it would be foolish to believe that evidence collected within one set of methodological rules or ideological framework cannot undergo secondary analysis for other purposes and from other theoretical perspectives; were that so, many historical records would be redundant. It is not necessary or useful for the practice of oral history to be uniquely tied to one epistemology or ideology. As with other archives of historical data, records of interviews will be used by researchers with many different theoretical viewpoints.

One of the most readily available theoretical critiques of oral history comes from the Birmingham Centre for Contemporary

Cultural Studies (hereafter the CCCS). Unfortunately it is embedded in a discussion of 'Popular Memory' (I have already made reference to this work) which they fail to distinguish from oral history, thus marginalizing much of their comment. Nevertheless, four issues relevant to the theory and purpose of oral history can be extracted from their work:

1   'The historian's empiricism is a real difficulty. It blocks political progress.'
2   'In what sense is individual witness evidence for larger social changes? How can these changes themselves be understood, not as something which evades human action, but also as the product of human labour, including this human personality?'
3   '[The difficulty is] . . . the tendency to identify the object of history as 'the past' . . . this definition cannot be held without a radical depoliticization of the practice of research. What is interesting . . . are not just the nuggets of 'fact' about the past, but the whole way in which popular memories are constructed and reconstructed as part of a *contemporary* consciousness.'
4   The problem of human relations in using these sources: the informant provides the information and the researcher uses it for his/her own professional advancement, and as the final interpreter the researcher assumes cultural and economic control of the 'joint' product.[1]

Point one, the depoliticizing of history by empiricism, and point four, the social relations of research, will be considered in the next chapter on 'purpose' in history.

Their second point considers an aspect of oral history methodology which is one of the concerns of this book, that is 'How can autobiographical materials be the source of, or contribute to, a more structural account of past and present?' They give a brief formulation of their position in distinguishing oral history from traditional biography, of which 'the main feature of much autobiographical writing is to *distinguish* the author from the people and the determinations that surround him'. Most autobiographies are published because, in some way, they are considered distinct from the ordinary. More than that, the underlying assumptions are of the free and self-willed individual of economic liberalism. From their perspective (and mine) a life history is valuable because it is informative about the social milieu rather than about a singular individual as such. People are shaped by their material and cultural world, and so individual experience is indicative of those processes. But this position ignores the problem, how typical is any individual account? For them, 'Representativeness, moreover, is a feature of social positions which are understood to be *shared* and *collective*.' They are representative not as the result of statistical practices but because, although each life is a unique sensory and psychological entity, its social determinations simply *are* shared by many others as a matter of reality. This is a variation of Ferrarotti's postulates about 'primary groups' and Sartre's 'singular universal'. It provides the basis for Bertaux's argument that no set number needs to be taken as a representative sample, one simply gets a saturation of knowledge from a contingent number of individual accounts from a specific milieu. Indeed, their assumptions appear to have much in common with the practices advocated in Chapter 10 on patterned responses.

In fact, if the practical implications are drawn from their theory they resemble the pragmatic materialism common to many historians. Let me cite from the introduction to a study of my own which used a good deal of oral evidence:

> . . . occupational, social and family life is a unified experience; more than that, those experiences are all facets of a unified socio-economic structure which shapes the relationship between those parts. . . . They enable us to perceive the real conjuncture of particular phenomena where much other evidence allows only inferences. The relationships which are apparent between different spheres of experiences in an open-ended interview *are real and known to coexist because they are simply facets of the one individual experience*, they are not the results of empirico-positivistic inductions nor specific 'data' collected to inform some preconception or theory. Analysis through grounded-theory from oral evidence has been called 'thick description', . . .[2]

Reference to 'thick description' comes from Peter Friedlander and indicates my debt to the introduction of his now classic study.[3] It is a practice which overlaps with that advocated by Bertaux and Ferrarotti. Friedlander's study of a branch of the United Automobile Workers was based almost entirely on the memory of Edmund Kord who was its president for most of its early years. The author and informant worked together for sixteen months and Kord commented on and corrected Friedlander's drafts. This cooperation demonstrates the value of oral evidence and how it allowed an understanding of events which would not have been possible by other means. Through his detailed knowledge and experience Kord revealed the importance of different age groups in the workforce and how their expectations of promotion, or lack of them, affected their attitudes, and how the different cultural and political backgrounds affected the attitudes and solidarities of the workforce. As Friedlander indicates, even if census data were available on the ethnic origins of the workforce it would be unlikely to help understand these effects because one needs to be aware that '. . . Lutheran Slovaks lived in a different cultural, political and social world than Catholic Slovaks, and that Bohemian Freethinkers were quite unlike both, the resulting category, Czechoslovak, is not only limited in its historical usefulness, but is misleading and mythological'. The 'limitations of depending on traditional sources' are that they are the result of previous abstractions: oral testimony takes us back to actual experience and lived differences and from which more appropriate categories can be evolved. Friedlander's analysis comes from what he describes as 'thick description' which 'projects a strategy of perception that is open-ended and concrete; whose dialectic seeks, not simplification and reduction to basic concepts, but elaboration and increasing complexity'. For him:

> What people were doing, rather than where (sociologically speaking) they were coming from, became my primary focus. . . . By focusing on practice rather than on sociological parameters it was possible to perceive coherent social formations whose activity and relationship to other formations exhibited an internal unity.[4]

In sum, his view is that one should avoid making *a priori* theoretical assumptions as 'The relationship of theory to description is essential'; thus Friedlander's approach is far more historical and constructive than the CCCS's, although one might assume that they would find elements of his approach sympathetic.

Certainly the strength and appeal of Friedlander's work is that it demonstrates the degree to which even a single interview can be used to illuminate socio-structural relationships and historical development. One does not have to have the resources for a large project in order to make a significant contribution to history through oral evidence. When dealing with the president of a union branch one is practising elite oral history in so far as the experience is unique. The issue of representativeness simply does not arise: on the other hand the problem of representativeness is not solved by such studies and their excellence should not be allowed to mask the issue. In criticism of Friedlander's work, it must be acknowledged that where he uses Kord to account for the activities and values of the various ethnic and cultural groups in the workforce his analysis is subject to serious internal theoretical contradictions. For Kord was a member of just one of those groups and by definition a product of that particular social and cultural milieu which Friedlander argues divides the workforce. As part of that divided workforce one must accept that, theoretically at least, his account must be partial and biased. One suspects that accounts from witnesses from the other ethnic groups, or factions in the union, might well give a rather different historical account. I would be very reluctant to accept as a rounded account the evidence of only one witness from within a situation which was ethnically and culturally complex. Given that Friedlander ascribes part of his own constructive relationship with Kord to their similar backgrounds then the potential for reinforcing a single perspective of a complex situation becomes quite worrying.

The limitation of the singular universal is precisely that it is the historical experience from one consciousness and however informative it may be it remains singular. The CCCS give a grudging acknowledgement of this without in any way accounting for how they would deal with the issue of representativeness: '. . . we must not assume that we have a perfect knowledge of what is typical before the accounts themselves emerge'.[5] Precisely, and the tendentious 'perfect' qualifying 'knowledge' does not disguise the fact that we do not have even a satisfactory knowledge of the parameters of many social phenomena in the recent past. One historical problem is to find evidence, and ways of using it, which would establish the distribution of cultural values, attitudes and practices of the great bulk of the population about which we have only the most fragmentary knowledge. This cannot come from postulating a general significance to every individual life history; it might come if a large enough sample from an archive, or number of archives, can be aggregated with some degree of confidence about their representativeness.

The main example for their critique is the work of Paul Thompson, not, as they make clear, because his work is any more at fault than that of other oral historians, but because he is one of its leading exponents and has been a major influence on its development. Yet it is Thompson who has been foremost in advocating the systematic collection and analysis of life histories in virtually the only way which has the potential to account for the distribution as well as the cause of historical experience from oral sources. When the CCCS critics ask '[from Thompson's theory] . . . some way of bridging the large-scale social processes which are the usual objects of historical accounts and the small-scale "private" narratives which are the very stuff of personal memories', their preconceptions prevent them from acknowledging his approach to it. They are, presumably, looking for something along the lines offered by Friedlander. I see nothing in Thompson's practice which would preclude the analysis of interviews from that perspective. It would simply answer different questions. Whatever method is used there is always a problem of accepting the testimony of an individual as an explanation of social processes: it exists whether the theoretical orientation is of Friedlander or Thompson. I could not discern how the CCCS proposed to resolve the problem. They claim that present practices (i.e. Thompson's) are too 'empirical' to allow this move from the individual to the social.

They also identify empiricism as the root of the ambivalence of whether the material should be used as the informant spoke it or as the researcher interprets it. In their view:

> . . . information about the past comes completely (sic) with evaluations, explanations and theories which often constitute a principal value of the account and are intrinsic to its representations of reality. Hence the feeling not uncommonly experienced in reading secondary interpretations of first accounts: we wish the bloody historian would go away and let us listen to the account itself! It seems more interesting, more nuanced, more complex and actually more explanatory than its secondary appropriation allows.

Most historians working with oral evidence are only too aware of the value and strength of the original interview, which is why they do not hypothesize about what people might say, but actually leave the campus in order to record people. It is why our definition of oral history included archiving the original recording, thus enabling others to listen to the informant directly for as long as such archives exist. But as historians we are also involved in using firsthand evidence for our own legitimate secondary analyses. As such we utilize various types of evidence and do not rely solely on one informant's unique perspective of the historical and socio-structural. The CCCS's position of accepting a single piece of testimony as 'more explanatory' is a curious one. The degree to which any account from an individual participant in society can be informative of the socio-structural depends to some degree on the listener's prior knowledge and conceptual framework. Some informants will describe their socio-structural view of the world, but in many cases this has to be deduced by whoever listens to it. One of the difficulties experienced by academics using oral history is that they do not want to appear elitist by interfering with the direct testimony and, genuinely, want to let informants' experiences and opinions shape our knowledge of history. But one should not be frightened of charges of elitism by pointing out that the people who can relate their experiences of a particular milieu are not always the same as the person most able to assess its historical significance. Many have spent a lifetime working to produce goods and services with other skills, and they would no more claim expertise in history than an historian or social scientist would as an electrician or tailoress. The informants do not offer a means by which their self-description might be combined with others from different social locations to form a more general historical analysis. Indeed, it is rather extraordinary to find that, having taken the position that the original text is most informative when the 'bloody historian' has not touched it, the CCCS then criticize Thompson[6] for presenting the oral evidence 'as a kind of unanalysable extra', in the 'raw' and for allowing informants to 'speak for themselves'. But how can historians satisfy them by 'going away' and letting others listen for themselves unless they allow the informant to 'speak for themselves'? There is a tension between the desire to interpret evidence from a variety of sources, including combining non-oral with oral, and the desire to preserve the integrity of the informant's personal account. The CCCS's own observations on the practice of 'bloody historians' does nothing to resolve or improve it.[7]

In pursuing their criticism of empirical practice as they see it, they draw a contrast between historical 'facts' and 'historically and socially constructed values'. But it is self-evident that the values and attitudes which any social group held at a particular time are as much 'facts' of history and as open to empirical investigation as are other human activities. Eventually they themselves are obliged to concede that this 'fact-value distinction is difficult to sustain', a concession which places a good deal of their own critique into question. Indeed, they go on to acknowledge that 'The subjective dimensions of human actions are as much "social facts" as externally observed behaviour'; they also eventually acknowledge that their position 'could apply to a range of theoretical and epistemological positions.' Thus they finally are obliged to end in much the same position that I have advocated in urging that oral history practice and evidence is not exclusively tied to any particular ideological position or theory of knowledge.

One can take a shortcut through some of their argument by perceiving that much of it depends on their view of how memory works. They assert that 'In memory past events, in their complexity, are worked and reworked' and, as we have already argued, this model of memory would leave little of historical value to be recalled. The status accorded to memory is fundamental. But having asserted memory as a reworked present consciousness, they modify this stance by acknowledging that 'Of course, there are also continuities and people do relive *certain* past events imaginarily, often with a peculiar vividness.' Their common sense on this point undermines their model of oral evidence as a product of contemporary consciousness. This may be the reason why they feel compelled to exaggerate the role of the interviewer as 'a further set of mediations' and put into the mouth of a hypothetical informant the line '. . . my answers are produced by *your* power'. They want to establish the position that contemporary power shapes and controls people's memories; but once they have conceded, however reluctantly, that recall of past events is possible then the dominant role of contemporary factors can be preserved only by reducing the informant's responses to the product of the present political, social and intellectual power structures. My experience of informants is that, although their responses may have been *elicited* by questions which reflected the areas of my interest, I have never had the *power* (nor the desire) to *produce* the answers. The scores of real people I have interviewed are made of rather less malleable clay than their hypothetical informant; and, in any case, if an oral history interview has been conducted according to the methods urged here it will also contain a considerable proportion of subject-matter determined by the informant. Indeed, it is difficult to reconcile their implications about the 'power' of the interviewer with their earlier conviction that the 'principal value' of these accounts is that they come with their own 'evaluations, explanations and theories' – the informants' ability to express these is hardly consistent with the notion of the historian's power to produce the informants' answers. The attitudes, values and personality of the interviewer will have *some* effect on what is said and how it is said; but to extend this factor to claim that material is 'produced' by the power of the interviewer is nonsense. The researcher is entirely dependent on the goodwill of the informant and the power relationship between the two is by no means a one-sided affair. As there are many levels of public and private discourse, so interviewers will collect interviews of varying levels, richness and depths. These will not only be affected by the informants' memories and their perception of the interviewer, but also by their descriptive and narrative ability. As it is acknowledged that the elderly are the most likely to have the type of memory which is particularly vivid and to 'relive', rather than 'reconstruct', past events oral historians working with them are more liable to collect authentic accounts than are contemporary researchers working with younger groups.

The CCCS's criticisms largely fail to engage with the practice of oral history because they discuss oral evidence and historians' use of it as if it were a self-enclosed theoretical world akin to those where an indeterminant number of angels of unknown size dance on pinheads. In fact, once an interview has been archived it becomes one more historical source for those who are not necessarily oral historians. The typescripts become documents in the way in which Mayhew's interviews have become documents. The process does not remain singular and contemporary.

13   Use and purpose

It gives history a future no longer tied to the cultural significance of the paper document. It also gives back to historians the oldest skill of their own craft.

Paul Thompson
The Voice of the Past (Oxford University Press 1978), p. 64

It is significant that the practice of oral history has created a ripple which has spread so widely. This is not, perhaps, surprising as, by the very nature of its source and generation, it requires the testimony of those whom history generally ignores. It challenges the unpeopled view of history which was epitomized by a river trip commentator who informed his listeners that 'On your left is Saint Paul's cathedral. It was built by Charles the Second with the help of Sir Christopher Wren' – without revealing which, if either, mixed the mortar or laid the stones.[1] We can now record how buildings are built and not rely only on architects' plans, or record all levels of a social whole rather than rely on the records of its formal institutions or leaders, where events are within living memory. This record is also more demotic in that it can be created by anyone with sufficient historical curiosity to want to add to the record, as it does not require any given level of literary skill. It brings professionals in touch with the experience of earlier decades in a way which documents or material artifacts do not; it also gives access to a range of information which has rarely been documented or preserved. It is unique in that it can be practised by anyone in virtually any location: one does not have to have access to a public record office or similar archive in order to be able to make an original contribution to the historical record. It is a method which has indeed cut history loose from the tyranny of the document and the institutions which generate them.

In the long run a change of method has more influence on history than a new interpretation of events. A new method changes the potential for new interpretations: new interpretations are superseded. As Paul Thompson argues:

> If the full potential of oral history is realized, it will result not so much in a specific list of titles to be found listed in a section of historical bibliographies, as in an underlying change in the way in which history is written and learned, in its questions and judgements, and in its texture.[2]

Part of his achievement is to have played a major role in establishing oral history as a professional tool while stimulating its use outside the universities. Because it has established links between academics and non-academics, and because of the information the oral method provides, it has attracted the attention and hopes of radicals. But there is a tendency to confuse radical historical practice with political radicalism. Because much working-class reminiscence is not particularly critical of the system – indeed, it often shows little overt concern with anything other than the personal – many social historians are disappointed with the testimony. As they are inhibited from criticizing the sources of what they perceive to be conservative oral evidence their criticism is focused on oral historians and the contemporary political significance of historical activity. The CCCS can again to be taken as an example, when they complain that the process of producing history from oral sources leaves untouched the '. . . first constructors of historical accounts . . .', that is, the informants. Once again it is not entirely clear what they want the historian to do, but it appears to involve entering into a dialogue with the informant and, by some means (presumably superior intellectual capital), obliging them to re-valuate their experience and to relate it as an overtly political position.[3] This approach must be utterly rejected. It would be totally dishonest to gain entry to informants' homes with the overt purpose of recording *their* account of life as they recall it through their own attitudes and values if the covert purpose was to alter their perspectives. Adding 'political education' to the process of interviewing would not enhance an understanding of the past, although I suspect that it would rapidly deplete the number of informants willing to be interviewed.

The CCCS may well be correct in asserting that '. . . a sense of history must be one element in a strong popular socialist culture'; but one must also acknowledge that not all historical inquiry is conducted by socialists and that oral history, which is a process of historical inquiry which listens to respondents of all political convictions, is not the exclusive location for such an activity. To go further and argue that ' Socialist popular memory today has to be a *newly constructed enterprise*: no mere recovery or re-creation is going to

do. Otherwise we shall find that nostalgia merely reproduces conservatism' is rather more disturbing.[4] It is not clear how one can
'newly construct' the past, nor how it could be made radical in areas
and at times when members of socialist groups could be counted in
tens and where even the Labour Party could not collect more than a
small fraction of the votes. Are they suggesting that a conservative
past be written out of the record or merely that one should exaggerate the numbers of the radical few? While the one-sided struggles of
pioneers should be recorded and celebrated, surely it is a much
more sensible *socialist* task to understand the roots and causes of
such conservatism and why socialism has not proved more appeal-
ing to the majority. It may not be the case as they assert that
'nostalgia reproduces conservatism' so much as 'conservatism reproduces conservatism': in any case historians should be trying to
understand the past rather than tailoring it to what they would have
liked it to be. But they are ultimately as unhappy with the idea that
the past exists as they were with the notion that people might recall
it: 'Again, the assumption that history anyway is about the past
encourages complicity with certain conservative nostalgia.'[5] It is
difficult for ordinary informants/oral historians to enter into a dialogue with this sort of perspective: no doubt our insistence that
something existed before present consciousness, and that it can be
related and recorded, must place intolerable restrictions on contemporary reshaping.

Oral historians are aware of these issues and Ken Worpole, who
has been centrally involved in promoting community publishing, is
himself critical of some of the simplistic assumptions surrounding it.
He writes of the apparent belief in some circles that if only all
aspects of every type of working-class experience could be recorded
the meaning of history might become clear; and even of a socialist
feeling that '. . . once every moment of past working-class experience has been noted and analysed, then all forms and structures of
capitalist relationships will powder and disintegrate leaving at last,
pure unmediated working-class authentic being'. His irony is jus-
tified. There is a danger that oral history could become a popular
equivalent of the earlier historical concern with every bit of trivia
about royalty and the rich; and while this might serve to strike a
justifiable balance, the result might simply be to add to the general
resources of conservative nostalgia. Recording life as it was in terms
of how much harder people worked, for less reward and longer
hours can hardly fail to show how comparatively better-off we are

now. Worpole reminds us that there should be some purpose in doing all this work. Much of the debate about oral history derives from varying opinions as to how well it fulfils the particular expectations of those who practise or comment on the activity. So many local history and reminiscence groups owe their existence to the enthusiasm and work of socialists, and oral history is an essential tool of such historical work. Even if workers lived close to good archival sources they would usually find little documentation relating to their lives. Oral evidence not only allows them the freedom to research their own history when and where they want to, it immediately gives them the status of expert witnesses even if they do nothing but record those experiences. But if a group carries through all the research up to publication then 'It is the study circle, discussion group, evening class – call it what you like – which best provides the context in which the study of history, local and national, can be socialized and politicized.'[6] It might be observed that such activities by local interest groups are not the preserve of any particular political or social group. Any group could use oral history for the history of their specific organization or area of interest: it is this potential power of the practice which provides its political potential. Stephen Yeo advances the point of view that for working people to be enabled to speak for themselves must, of itself, be a political act:

> History looks different, IS different from different points of view, different locations, different class positions. Any reports of length, depths and authenticity from . . . [the voiceless] however disconcerting, are correspondingly golden. A sense of time, place and connection *is* revolutionary.[7]

Well, I agree about the importance of the information recorded by the voiceless, and I agree that historical experience is reported differently from the class experience of the informants, but I am not convinced that it is revolutionary in itself. It depends on the time, place and connections which the informant has lived through and this can give some people a sense of the rightness of privilege and an unjustified sense of their own humbleness. Perhaps the most widespread sense (common sense) that I have encountered in the oral testimonies or ordinary people is one of powerlessness and the necessity to accept 'things as they were' rather than to feel militant about things as they 'might have been'.

As with any other form of historical evidence it is the manner in which it is interpreted and used which gives it significance. Perhaps the clearest example of this comes from the immensely successful American author Studs Terkel (who has probably done as much as any man to bring oral history to public attention), one of whose books, *Hard Times*,[8] contains over one hundred and fifty interview extracts from the experience of ordinary Americans focusing on the 1930s. Its impact was perceptively reviewed by Michael Frisch[9] who was struck by the fact that, as testimony from a period when the capitalist economic and financial system almost collapsed and through its failings plunged millions of Americans into acute distress, the book's contents were received with acclaim as a 'huge anthem of praise of the American spirit'. This was because economic failure and the inadequate political response to it were related from the perspective of the individual as personal experiences of good or bad luck, of being comparatively better or worse off than others, or similar categories within which raw experience is commonly understood. The accounts are moving comment on humanity because they show the fortitude and resilience of ordinary people subjected to hardship and stress, but there is very little in terms of an overt critique of the system which plunged decent people into such misery. Because individual oral testimony largely obscures the importance of structural forces the CCCS oral history group label this tendency 'humanism', and they are correct in identifying this as one of the major pitfalls in using oral evidence. Accounts of work are central to most people's experience and, in the realm of most paid labour, it takes place collectively for the profit and purposes of others. How a society produces its good and services is the basis upon which much else, especially social differences, are built and maintained. The quietist flavour of much oral evidence, observed by the CCCS, has also been commented upon by oral historians, in this case using work experience as an example:

> Work is treated very much as if it were a thing complete in itself, instead of being one part of a social relationship: we do it because we do it. The dignity of labour, stressed by many of the local oral histories which focus on work, disguises what work is for – who owns what we produce, where profits come from, why we are deprived of work, how new jobs are made, the social consequences of the things we do, and so on.[10]

I share this view that oral evidence and the practice of recording interviews is not in itself a radical activity. It provides one-sided evidence of the lives of labour but not the movements of capital. It is a method which can provide very detailed accounts of wages, but is silent on the question of profits; and can inform us how that wage was consumed domestically, but not where the profits were reinvested. Given that so many dimensions of economic life occur at the level of institutional, national and international finance and of technology it is not surprising that those aspects are not recorded in most oral accounts.

This is an obvious limitation of oral evidence, just as the statistical evidence which shows the movements of capital are limited in not demonstrating the human results of those movements: no historian would expect any one source of evidence to provide a rounded picture of the period. The objection to oral evidence on the grounds of 'humanism' is not sustainable where it is a part of a wider historical activity. One can even agree that most people relate their experiences through the

> . . . personalities of employers (slave-driving, posh and distant, or 'reasonable') and on the qualities of forepersons or workmates. The character of a person is seen as making an immense difference to working experience, the difference between a good job and a bad.[11]

However, one does not have to accept the CCCS's objection to it as a form of false consciousness or as a defect in the evidence. From my own experience as a manual worker between 1944 and 1963 I know that those 'humanist' distinctions are made with good cause. There are good and bad employers, some forepersons did turn a blind eye to practices which make the working day more pleasant or profitable, and those people did change people's perceptions of exploitation. That was not 'false consciousness', for how a system is applied does make a material difference to how it is experienced. It is more constructive to allow the informants the credit of knowing the authenticity of their own experience instead of wishing that they were more obviously class-conscious. Most people (for whatever reasons of material and cultural domination) live in a world in which the circumstances of their life are made more or less tolerable by the way power and authority are exercised by other people; that is how they experienced their life and that is how they relate it.

An understanding of industrial, political and social responses, or the values and attitudes which coexisted with them, will not come from attempting to indoctrinate informants into changing their testimony. Informants have the right to their own memories of the past, as Frisch writes about the 'humanist' testimonies in *Hard Times*:

> Anyone who has wondered why the depression crises did not produce more focused critiques of American capitalism and culture, more sustained efforts to see fundamental structural change, will find more evidence in the interior of these testimonies than in any other source I know.[12]

In other words the apparent limitations of individual testimony is one reason why oral evidence is theoretically as well as empirically useful. Because it expresses individual perspectives it provides a crucial insight into how people experience exploitative systems while generally deriving enjoyment from their lives, and how their industrial, cultural and political values allow the status quo to continue. Indeed, the actual shape and form of the narrative is in itself a clear statement of the level of political development of the informant. There is bound to be a conservative tendency on the surface of most oral evidence when it is simply published in biographical form or as fragments of such. One cannot achieve a radical aim simply by publishing individual experience because individual categories remain the framework of interpretation and so reinforce the perception of the historical process as an atomic rather than a social process. This tendency is reinforced where the evidence is taken from only one section of material and social experience and, although there are those who scarcely consider elite oral history as being part of the oral history movement, the testimony of elites offers the opportunity to throw some light on the administration of power. Oral evidence is incomplete in itself, it is even more partial to imagine that the history of a class society can be written from evidence drawn from only one section of it. It is for these reasons that I feel that to simply let oral evidence stand in its autobiographical form is to betray the contribution to the historical record which such evidence can make: to realize its potential it must be related to the testimony of others and triangulated with documentary and material evidence. I have always made it clear to people that I was not interviewing them as 'biographical' figures, but for their contribution to our knowledge of the material and social conditions of the period through which they have lived. I cannot express my own position better than the words of Peter Burke:

> . . . I should like to say that (although I consider myself a socialist and a historian), I'm not a socialist historian; that is I don't believe in

socialist history. I believe that to use history as a weapon in political struggle is counter-productive. One comes to believe one's own propaganda, to overdramatise the past, and hence to forget the real complexity of the issues at any one time.[13]

The activities of socialist historians apart, I believe that there is a greater danger of the present being screened through the past than of the past through the present. This conclusion has grown in me from listening to kin as well as through more formal research. There has been a great deal of concern over the degree to which the past gets distorted through being related in the present, yet oral historians have paid much less attention to the effect of the past on the present. This is not surprising given that the past is the focus of their concern, although the role of the national 'past' in legitimizing conservatism in the present has been perceptively argued by the CCCS. Personal memory can also work to create a conservative view of the present, and Jerry White reports coming to this same perception that '. . . one of the dangers in the oral history/ autobiography project is not so much a romanticisation of the past, but the romanticisation of the present'. He refers to Peter Townsend's work which shows that '. . . some of today's poor deny the existence of poverty, and use the past as a direct reference point . . .' to establish that hardship was worse in days gone-by and that people today should not complain because life is better 'now' than 'then'.[14] The perception that things have got better is certainly a powerful conservative current. For example, I recall one occasion when my own family was admiring the final year's school work of a young cousin, the school-leaving age being fifteen at the time. The conversation turned to education in general and the observation that I would have enjoyed an extra year instead of leaving at fourteen. This was compared in turn with my mother leaving at thirteen years of age and my grandmother at twelve. From there the discussion moved to the amount of work children had been obliged to do both at home and for wages: my mother for example, living-in as a domestic servant during her last year of schooling. The general consensus of these recollections what that to have a longer childhood with more play and less work was an improvement on the past. The 'truth' of such observations need not concern us, but for the last two generations it is a fact of experience that in terms of fewer hours of toil, better leisure facilities, higher standards of comfort and a whole range of directly experienced dimensions the quality of life has undoubtedly improved for the majority of families. That people experience satisfaction in witnessing the improvement in their lives and those of their descendants imparts a generalized political satisfaction with the system within which this has happened.

At the moment there is no certain relationship in the bias between changes in past and present; none, at least, which might be theorized with any confidence. The return of mass unemployment from the late 1970s could change the present effect as informants in the future might recall their past as a 'Golden Age' which could provide a radical reference point for a critique of the present. The sort of inbuilt biases and distortions that one is liable to find in oral evidence will certainly change as the material distinctions between past and present change. Any conceptualization of the radical/ conservative potential of oral evidence must be historical and dialectical if it is to provide an adequate methodological critique.

The difficulty with the desire to give people back their history is that most people do not have one, they have personal memories. Any conception they have of history is derived from schooling, the media and the 'historic' buildings and material remains they may see around them. Many informants feel excluded from history and, when interviewed, will frequently attempt to recall memories of royal marriages, coronations and deaths, national events such as war service and, less often, notable local events. They have to be convinced that their experience is part of history and to be encouraged to talk in detail about their own lives. The CCCS are correct in arguing that history, as presented as a national past, does exercise contemporary power over the *voluntary* recollections of informants. The drawback lies less in distorting those memories, however, than in denying them a role in history, and part of the constructive role of the oral historian lies precisely in seeking-out people who would not otherwise record their historical experience. The crucial distinction between autobiographical and interview materials is that the latter is the product of two people not one: because an interview is not a narrative it gains in value.

The purpose of oral history should be to improve and enlarge the practice of history. If the criticism over the overt political and cultural use of oral evidence is now left aside only the alleged limitations of 'empirical' oral history practice remain to be considered. This limitation, as we have argued above, is inherent in the individual nature of experience given in the initial account. It follows that any raw data aggregated from such accounts must suffer similar limitations and will not reveal the global attributes of social action; a sufficient number, however, could reveal the morphology of historically experienced attitudes and activities coexisting with material cultures. This, however, does not weaken the case for oral history or the practices advocated; it simply reiterates the point that oral history is not a self-contained sub-field but another source of historical information to be used in as many ways as are constructive. There are a number of ways of approaching this but one cannot ignore the contribution of sheer factual 'thick' description. It is impossible to understand, for example, how low-paid male workers managed to provide for large families from documents on wages and prices. Yet even one informant can illuminate the process, and how it relates to family networks and community practices, by recording the family economy in the round: how the spouse contributed to the family standard-of-living by making and repairing clothes; preserving jams, pickles and other foods; earning cash from casual and seasonal work of all kinds. In addition, children contributed through waged and unwaged labour in a myriad of jobs, as baby minders, errand boys, mothers' helps and so forth. Had the breadwinner been the sole contributor to the family budget or the spouse the sole domestic toiler, then there would have been even less bread or comfort than existed.

It is within these recalled material situations that the political and social values, attitudes and activities of both the individual and their immediate social milieu can be understood. There are good reasons for supposing that the family could be the best unit for considering both society and the individual as suggested by Ferrarotti: the 'singular universal' is a concept which transcends the individualistic source of oral testimony. But whatever the unit of analysis or the method used the actual recall of the material and cultural dimensions of experience are a necessary bedrock from which to understand how people experienced history. It is, in any case, an inescapable fact that it is within these personal contexts that most people relate their experience. Given that in any past period only a tiny minority have been activists it is unrealistic to expect the testimony to contain much activist experience. Most criticism of the *status quo* will have to emerge from the use to which the basic experience is put, by, for example, taking a 'poor but happy' life story and illustrating the level of exploitation which is a 'silence' within the account. Many interviews have critical messages in so far as they reflect the waste of human potential implicit in the limited horizons and low expectations created by material experience. Oral techniques provide a means of recovering historical information and if it is especially useful for capturing the voice of the disregarded it must be remembered that it is equally at home recording elite history.

The final point of the CCCS's demands from oral history which we noted related to 'the social relations of research', and this has been implicit in much of the preceding comment about sharing with informants the production of historical knowledge through community and political activity. In essence it is largely a question of relative cultural power between classes and, more narrowly, between the informant and the historian. This is an issue which applies to all intellectual production and, as far as oral history is concerned, is something of a transitory issue. I have already expressed the view that critics outside oral history have an exaggerated idea of the power of interviewers to influence the answers they receive from informants. But I would make clear that I am not suggesting that interviewers should pretend to be apolitical or to avoid sensitive political or social issues, only that interviewers should always remain conscious of the fact that the prime point of the exercise is to obtain the opinions of the informant. There may be occasions when expressing a political stance is advantageous, such as when interviewing someone who has been actively involved in a particular cause. Such a person will often be more inclined to open up to a sympathizer, although even in these cases where the interviewer gains something from an overt political stance there are disadvantages. Faced with another activist in the same cause an informant might well be more anxious to justify the 'correctness' of their work in the light of contemporary views within the movement than to record the events as they remember them; whereas someone they perceive as sufficiently well-informed to appreciate the significance of what they are relating could obtain a better historical account simply because they will not be perceived as a critical evaluator of what is said but merely as a recorder of it. I am not arguing here for 'value-free' history but simply indicating that the cultural norms within which we conduct our interviews ensure that the informants are going to express their own views more openly if they are aware that we are not committed to collecting a particular version of events. It serves the collection of historical data better if interviewers do not force their own position to the attention of the informant: oral historians do not go to their informants to educate them, but to be informed by them.

The social relations in oral history are also transitory. No matter

what degree of collective activity is involved in the original interpretation it is not engraved on tablets of stone – and if it were, it
would still be reinterpreted at later dates. Given that many interviews are with the over-seventy age group few informants have a
long life expectancy – and even historians are mortal – so even if oral
history were to be generated under some form of egalitarian community control it would soon become a public source for anyone
who wishes to use it for secondary analysis. In this it is no different
from diaries, letters and other personal documents which enter the
public domain through various contingencies not foreseen or provided for by the originators. Oral evidence rapidly becomes simple
historical evidence.

Nevertheless, the social relations of oral history offer the elderly
a status which age and experience no longer command so readily as
in the past. The practical experience of elderly workers may no
longer offer valuable precedents in a world where technology has
replaced the methods in which they were experienced; but their
historical knowledge is unique to their age and location. This does
enhance their self-esteem, and when I have expressed my thanks
and debt to them at the end of an interview I have had them thank
me for enabling them still to feel useful and, although perhaps
bedridden, still be able to make a contribution to society. Indeed,
the human relations involved in oral history have spilled well
beyond the bounds and practices of historians. The process of interviewing a person to collect their previous experience is a social process
by no means restricted to the practice of history; it is used in other
areas which may well be even more rewarding for those involved.

As personal recollections are also an essential part of our sense of
who and what we are now, historical recall is being used as therapy
for elderly people who are confused or withdrawn. Age Concern[15]
has developed a system of reminiscence packs which contain tapes
of popular songs of an earlier period and accounts from people of an
earlier generation talking about their younger days. These act as a
focus for reminiscence groups. One great advantage of this
approach is that local groups could produce tapes relevant to their
particular locality and through their specificity stand a better chance
of stirring the memory and gaining a response from any particular
individual. The experience of Norris and Eilah is interesting in this
respect; they had a group of elderly people in institutional care
talking about the past: '. . . in some instances several of the otherwise mute or confused members could be observed asking questions

of others and generally providing the momentum and direction for the group's interaction.'[16] This also helped the nurses to have a more constructive interaction with the patients in the daily routine outside of the group's meetings, because they learned about the patients' former lives and could then respond to that human record and no longer perceive patients simply as senile and incontinent bodies to be physically cared for in the present. They even had a reminiscence outing to visit familiar surroundings, and at least one profound depressive responded to his old workplace with a smile. The authors emphasize that the practice is no cure for senility, but that it can be a palliative and a stimulus to many elderly people who are beginning to lose their grip of reality. This sort of therapy shows the importance of the ability to recall personal experience lived through specific times and locations for the mental health of individuals If we are what genetics and society has made us, we are (whatever the role of the subconscious) also substantially what we remember of that process.

Oral history is also growing in the schools and in radio programmes, and is providing the substance of drama. In fact as one practitioner has written:

> We are just beginning to see the impact that oral history can have on different areas of the school curriculum. Drama offers a rare opportunity for pupils to explore issues of value relating to important social and political topics and oral history can inform this process.[17]

The rich store of social and historical experience held in the memories of people in all walks of life is history. It is, or should be, recorded and used in a range of educational and cultural forms, and I welcome whatever variety of constructive use other disciplines and professions might find for recorded recall. But however agreeable it may be for oral history to have such constructive facets to offer society, they are separate fields; historians as such are not psychiatrists nor social workers concerned with the mental health of the elderly, nor, for that matter, dramatists. These activities are very desirable in themselves and it is socially valuable for oral historians to be associated with them; but their concerns are not those of historical record or accuracy.

As individuals our contact with others will reflect our social self, but in so far as we are historians our concern is with the historical value of such contact and that lies through the methodology and practice of oral history.

14 Conclusion

> . . . people in houses . . . lived in the middle of their legacies and presents, and each piece of furniture is a memento. . . . they have kept everything. The past is a luxury of ownership.
>
> Where then should I keep mine? One cannot put one's past in one's pocket; one must have a house in which to keep it.[1]

Jean-Paul Sartre
La nausée, Folio (Saint-Amand 1972), pp. 96–7

Preservation is a prerequisite for entering the historical record. By preserving memories oral history redresses the balance of experience against artifacts, and although it records the experience of all, it is especially valuable in preserving the history of those whose material possessions have been meagre, contemporary and transitory. They have not kept their past in their houses or their pockets, but in their heads. It is a method which can place on permanent record anyone's historical experience: its limitation is that of living memory. For these reasons it is a major transformation of the historical record and through that, of historical practice. It has made history more demotic both in terms of those who record it, and those whose experience is recorded. As with all historical records, however, it needs to be properly analysed and interpreted.

History has ever been a quarry for poets, painters, dramatists, politicians, moralists, novelists and so on – indeed, as history is the collective record of our human experience it is difficult to conceive how it could be otherwise. Because it is an activity which involves living people the use of oral history methods has extended these activities as far as therapy for the old. These uses are a welcome part of the value of historical knowledge. I started, however, with a definition of oral history practice which was centrally concerned with the contribution which the recall method can make to historical knowledge – and that has been the focus of the text. Those other uses are well represented in the journal of the Oral History Society and as themes for its conferences. But such uses have their own

purposes which are not necessarily congruent with how the recorded recall of personal experience might best contribute to the
authenticity of history, which is our central concern. As such, oral
evidence has to be carefully collected and painstakingly analysed;
and here I make no distinction between practitioners whether they
be individuals recording only their own family history, local history
groups of whatever size and persuasion, or the large projects funded
at museums and universities; all have an interest in considering
which practice will give the most authentic evidence.

The value of oral evidence as a historical source must ultimately be
established within its own authenticity. If it is accepted as authentic
only when confirmed by documentary sources then one might as
well use the documents. Debating the superiority of either
documentary or oral evidence is essentially sterile because both
have their strengths and weaknesses. Contemporary documents
have their 'silences' as often as oral evidence. The value of each can
be enhanced when used with the other because they have been set
down at different times and were subject to different personal
biases, contemporary pressures and social conventions. They
should be used to illuminate the defects of one another rather than
be seen as simple contradictions. Historians of elite groups have
shown the greatest scepticism about oral evidence, and social historians are its main protagonists. This is not surprising or a reflection
on the methods or rigour of either activity. The nature of the
historical problem affects the contribution which personal recollections can make to its resolution; and oral evidence, to date, has
made a greater contribution to social history than political. This is
partially due to the relationship between memory and activity, and
the paucity of adequate documentation for large areas of social
history; but also to a greater professional predisposition to accept
the 'truth' of documents rather than the oral, which stems from
familiar practice rather than rational assessment of the respective
merits. The essential position for oral historians is to ensure that the
authenticity of any source be scrutinized as sceptically as is oral
evidence. Contemporary documents are produced within the pressures and biases of the day, they are produced for a purpose, which
may well be to dissimulate, persuade, or at least, put a gloss on a
real situation. One of our few certainties can be that many contemporary documents, especially those generated by some elites, are
not intended to reflect the literal truth.

Oral history may be essentially about individual experience, but it is not biographical in intent. The method is, at bedrock, the stimulation of personal recall by a historical researcher seeking information for a social interpretation. This tension between the individual and the social is at the heart of most of the ambiguities, difficulties and different schools of thought within oral history. Its strength is that it is a coherent source, in that connections are real and known because they are united in the one experience and have not been assumed through methodological induction or theoretical construction. It is on the basis of this unity that some researchers disregard the issue of representative sampling as understood by positivistic social science. They argue that causal connections and social relations are apparent from pursuing a strategic sample to an informational saturation point. This is valid in terms of specific research, but to accept it as the full extent to which oral evidence can contribute to history would be unduly self-restricting. If there are enough interviews of known sociological provenance then oral evidence can contribute to a morphological understanding of historical phenomena.

How representative one life may be of others remains a basic issue to which there is no single answer; at best there are degrees of credibility which could be applied to each level of generality. The more constrained the circumstances of an experience the more liable it is to be typical of others. If memories of National Service life are taken as an example, accounts of the initial training at a given camp would all be much more similar than accounts of subsequent service as men were posted to different regiments, bases and countries. The same principle applies to all the cases. The experience of the bricklayer will have a higher probability of being typical of a particular locality than of a region or of bricklayers nationally: it would be even less typical of the experience of 'skilled craftsmen', because as categories become more general the range of experience they encompass is more varied. It is a simple principle, but one which has not always sufficiently observed when evaluating the validity of particular types of historical evidence. So although there is a level of historical authenticity in each interview the issue is a matter of having sufficient interviews from which to generalize about particular historical categories, localities and periods. This is why it is crucial to consider the question of samples and how one gains sufficient confidence to generalize.

A distinction has been made between the practice of planning samples to ensure that a representative sample of experience is collected, and the strategic approach in which informants from a particular occupation or category are interviewed until 'saturation point' is reached. I find these approaches less antithetical than some of their practitioners. My research on the East Anglian fishermen was planned as a sample in order to ensure that the variety of experience was collected; on the other hand, as it was focused on a single occupation it could be viewed as a strategic sample which reached a satisfactory point of saturation. Clearly, in terms of particular research projects either approach can lead to much the same result in terms of who is selected for interview. Nevertheless, I feel that the perspective of sampling offers the more constructive framework for cumulative historical work. The defect of strategic interviewing is that it is essentially researcher orientated and informants are used to provide an understanding of a specific issue rather than as singular universals with a comprehensive experience to relate. This is quite legitimate in terms of a specific research problem but it reduces the value of the interviews for any secondary analysis or future use as part of an archive of interviews. While one would acknowledge that any research will have its own specific focus and could not cover all aspects of a person's life in the same detail, where each informant is conceived as a potential contribution to a larger sample for general historical research there is some pressure to treat each one as comprehensively as resources allow.

It might also be acknowledged that sampling is not a practical problem for much oral history work; after all, if one is using interviews to record family history the 'population' and the 'sample' are liable to amount to much the same thing. This would also be true if research was aimed at collecting oral evidence on a community, institution or occupation as far back in time as memory can go; clearly one simply interviews the most elderly informants one can trace. I have argued for an awareness of sampling, however, as much for its contribution to *post hoc* analysis as to actually finding and choosing informants. If one is aware of the sample size and shape needed to give a complete picture of a community one will be aware of the areas of experience where one has not found informants. Being aware of the gaps can prove the stimulus to actually finding the appropriate informants to interview.

The interview itself is, in one sense at least, the real pivot of the practice because it is during this process that the informants communicate their experience for the record. Fortunately for us all, once they have been prompted to talk about specific aspects of their life many informants will do so with sufficient clarity to save interviewers from the worst of their failings. Because the informant is making a constructive contribution and is not treated as simply a 'response' to a limited question one can dismiss much of the social survey analysis of the interviewing process. Perhaps 'dismiss' overstates the case slightly as there is no doubt that the identities of the interviewer and of the informant and the relationship between them will affect the information which is collected. And that is, theoretically at least, a substantial issue. If people give different accounts to different people which one should be taken as authentic? The common sense answer is that one needs to be aware of the areas and subjects which have not been discussed. But there is the additional complication that the informant is liable to place different evaluations on his or her life at different times. An account of family life and the attitudes and evaluations of early experience are liable to change as one's own experience matures. For this reason the activities rather than evaluations are crucial: the material conditions of life will be reported more consistently than the evaluations of them. By all means collect the latter, but appreciate that they are changeable, and that they are more liable to be only partially expressed, modified or concealed in response to the perceived personality, gender and class of the interviewer than are accounts of the simple material experience. It is also important to bear in mind the age of the informant at the time they experienced a set of circumstances. One major limitation of oral evidence is that childhood memories are simply that, the memories of a child who could not have been aware of all the problems of adult life. This does not mean that the information is unreliable, simply that it has that limitation.

Good interviewing is about communication and it is the interviewer's responsibility to ensure that the informant's account is historically valuable. It is not enough for the informant to express a view of the 'rich'; to be useful that personal category needs to be related to a public category such as the aristocracy or the professional middle class on a national scale, or to the local social structure, and preferably to both. Individuals will designate even clerical workers as rich, and it requires conscientious interviewing to ensure that the informant's world view and their social boundaries are clearly understandable. It is a delusion to believe that one has understood informants if it is not possible to integrate their various terminology to a common meaning. One of the major difficulties with (bad) interviews is that it is often difficult to understand what is meant from what has been said. I have put the view that communication will be better where the sort of questions which will establish such boundaries have been pre-planned in a schedule ready to use where necessary. Nevertheless, I have also acknowledged that much valid information comes tangentially from different contexts and that answers to direct questions are often found to be erroneous as the interview proceeds. This is not so much an argument against detailed questioning as against the notion that we invariably get a valid answer to a direct question in the way survey methodology assumes. It is the detailed prompting with prepared questions on details of life which actually extract the valid corrections. To leave the informants to tell what they will is to abdicate all contribution to the interview. Memory often needs to be made to work and one of the major advantages of questions is that they stimulate detailed recall and get beyond the surface generalities. This is part of my objection to the type of strategic interviewing which suggests that some questions and areas of discussion can be dropped as the researcher gains saturation of knowledge on simple aspects of the daily routine in order to concentrate on the more complex relationships: such a process abandons the main means of stimulating the recall which would provide a more authentic account of such relationships.

Now that computers are so widely used in libraries and archives to permit rapid and precise access to information it is clear that oral evidence will require this processing if it is to be widely used. The coding of open-ended interviews has been dismissed as undesirable because of the qualitative nature of the material and the positivistic assumptions inherent in categorical coding; but coding does not prevent anyone from using the full qualitative interview if they wish. I argue for the value of such coding on a number of grounds – and not least the qualitative improvement in the interviews which can result from it. Trying to categorize an interview is the surest way of revealing ambiguities, omissions, silences, contradictions and all the myriad failings to which most forms of communication are open. Such an exercise (on even one interview) would improve the material collected by most people. It is also constructive historically as the researchers realize which areas they need to cover more carefully, and it can also expose gender assumptions in the research or interviews as it becomes clear that certain areas are fully covered for one sex but not the other.

Not that the use of oral evidence in archives is only a matter of exposing failings in technique. Through its systematic use it should be possible to question basic assumptions and to construct better categories. For example the experiences of the working class are almost invariably analysed through the tripartite categories of skilled, semi-skilled and unskilled. But it is evident that these categories are only moderately successful in dividing the social, political and cultural experience of the working class. The nature of the occupation, income, the availability of work for spouses and young children, the level of rents, the cost of food and services in the locality, are only a few of the factors besides skill which determine material and social life. Skill is a very poor guide to any social experience – for example, handloom weavers were no less skilled in the 1840s than they had been previously but this did little for their material conditions save, perhaps, make them worse. Because oral evidence is such a unified source when collected with due regard to sampling and systematic interviewing, it holds the potential to examine actual experience and to establish a wide range of criteria by which to establish better categories. This is a difficult task but essential if social history is going to escape from the dead hand of nineteenth-century occupational categories. Social history will not contribute what it might to historical analysis until it is prepared to listen to the voices of experience from different social levels and to work from their original material. Oral evidence is exciting, humanistic and one of the most rounded sources of history: but it is also an exacting and challenging form of historical record and not an easy option which can be left to speak for itself.

Notes on the text

Chapter 1   Introduction

1   I repeat that this does not include technical advice on recorders or recording technique. As equipment is continually improving advice of this sort can rapidly become dated and it might be as well simply to take Margaret Brooks' word that the '. . . IASA (the International Association of Sound Archives), the Imperial War Museum and BIRS (the British Institute of Recorded Sound, now the National Sound Archive) are generally eager to encourage oral history, and are pleased to give advice on equipment, materials and techniques to interested fellow practitioners.' Information from these sources will always be up-to-date and of high quality. Reference to Chapter 5 of Anthony Seldon and Joanna Pappworth, *By Word of Mouth: Elite Oral History* (Methuen 1983), p. 93.

Chapter 2   Origins and potential

1   Paul Thompson, *The Voice of the Past* (Oxford University Press 1978).
2   For examples of this, and a variety of subjects and topics using oral history see, Paul Thompson (ed.) *Our Common History: The Transformation of Europe* (Pluto Press 1982).

Chapter 3   Definition

1   Willa K. Baum, 'Oral History in the United States', *Oral History*, **1**, no. 3, Autumn 1972, p. 16.
2   Seldon and Pappworth, p. 71.
3   Jan Vansina (translated by H. M. Wright), *Oral Tradition* (Routledge & Kegan Paul 1965). This is the classic account of this form of historical evidence, its uses and difficulties. For a more recent example see Andrew Roberts, 'The use of Oral

Sources for African History' in *Oral History*, **4**, no. 1, Spring 1976.

4   Paul Thompson, 'Oral History in North America', *Oral History*, **3**, no. 1, Spring 1975, p. 33.

Chapter 4   The informants

1   Roderick Floud, *An Introduction to Quantitative Methods for Historians* (Methuen 1973), p. 162. This is a useful starting point for some simple examples and the application of sampling to historical data. The most convenient source to pursue sampling theory is any of the encyclopedias of the Social Sciences.

2   Trevor Lummis, *Occupation and Society: The East Anglian Fishermen 1880–1914* (Cambridge University Press 1985). My observations on the drinking habits of the fishermen had some documentary confirmation.

3   This initial project *Family Life and Work Experience before 1918* was followed by *Middle and Upper Class Families in the early Twentieth Century* and *The Family and Community Life of East Anglian Fishermen in the late nineteenth and early twentieth century*. Although each had a specific focus the two subsequent projects were designed to be compatible with the first. All three were directed by Paul Thompson. The archive has had numerous other additions.

4   Jane Synge, 'Cohort Analysis in the Planning and Interpretation of Research Using Life Histories', in Daniel Bertaux (ed.), *Biography and Society* (Sage 1981), p. 236.

5   Synge, p. 237.

6   Synge, p. 236.

Chapter 5   The interview schedule

1   A. N. Oppenheim, *Questionnaire Design and Attitude Measurement* (Heinemann 1966). Although rather dated this is a source I found clear and comprehensible.

2   There are exceptions to this and some social surveys allow one or two questions with open answers, but as the interviewer has to write them down while listening to the comments one might wonder at the accuracy of these responses.

3   The best source for understanding the variety of oral history

research is to consult *Oral History: The Journal of the Oral History Society*, which is published biannually by the Oral History Society. It publishes articles from oral historians worldwide and news of oral history developments internationally. It is sent to all members of the society: details of membership and the address for all correspondence is: Oral History, Department of Sociology, University of Essex, Colchester CO4 3SQ, England.

Chapter 6   The interview

1   Robert Bogdan and Steven J. Taylor, *Introduction to Qualitative Research Methods: a Phenomenological Approach to the Social Sciences*, New York (John Wiley & Sons 1975), p. 138.
2   Essex Oral History Archive (EOHA), interview no. 3011, p. 16. I thank its director Paul Thompson for permission to publish these and subsequent extracts.
3   EOHA, no. 245, p. 5.
4   EOHA, no. 225, pp. 4 and 44.
5   EOHA, no. 145, pp. 6 and 49.
6   John Saville, 'Oral History and the Labour Historians', *Oral History*, **1**, no 3, Autumn 1972, pp. 60–2.
7   E. P. Thompson, 'On History, Sociology and Historical Relevance', *British Journal of Sociology*, **27**, no. 3, September 1976. A review essay of Robert Moore, *Pit-Men, Preachers and Politics* (Cambridge University Press 1974).

Chapter 7   The single interview: documentary confirmation

1   For example, *The Annual Reports of the Inspector of Sea Fisheries*.
2   EOHA, no. 3035, p. 22.
3   EOHA, no. 3045, pp. 7 and 40.
4   The range of historical questions which can be asked of census data obviously depends on the questions set by a particular census.
5   For an example of the use of oral testimony in this context see Isabelle Bertaux-Wiame, 'The Life-History Approach to the Study of Internal Migration', Bertaux (ed.): 1981.
6   EOHA, no. 3025. pp. 60–1. An account of the suicide appears in *The Lowestoft Journal*, 22 June 1901.

7   EOHA, no. 3025.
8   EOHA, no. 261.
9   EOHA, no. 3010. *The Lowestoft Journal*, 27 November 1909, reports a case of two boys using such pistols to rob a market stall, and on 4 January 1913 a report which notes one person killed by these weapons specifically distinguishes them from air-guns.
10 Seldon and Pappworth, p. 18.
11 Brian Harrison, 'Oral History and Recent Political History', *Oral History*, **1**, no. 3, Autumn 1972, p. 37.
12 Ibid., p. 38.
13 H. Butterfield, *History and Human Relations* (Collins 1951), p. 199.

Chapter 8   The single interview: internal consistency

1   George Edwards, *From Crow-Scaring to Westminster* (The Labour Publishing Company Ltd. 1922).
2   Bogdan and Taylor, 1975.
3   EOHA, no. 225.
4   Janet Gyford, 'Shop People and their Customers: Witham, Essex, 1900–39', unpublished M.A. Oral History Project, Department of Sociology, University of Essex, 1981.
5   Bernard Waites, 'The Language and Imagery of "Class" in Early Twentieth-Century England (Circa 1900–1925)', *Literature and History*, **4**, 1976, p. 37.
6   EOHA, no. 3014, p. 48; and no. 3057, p. 18.
7   Robert Tressell, *The Ragged Trousered Philanthropists*, (Panther 1965). This is the first unabridged edition. The author was a working painter and the novel describes the lives of a group of painters and decorators in Hastings around 1906.
8   Personality bias may have been at work here in so far as he was the youngest person I interviewed at that day centre, and he may have been trying to show himself more knowledgeable about an earlier period than his age warranted. In those circles age confers status.

Chapter 9   Aggregating data

1   My discussion is limited to the *historical* use of such material and how a number of interviews extend interpretation. Archiv-

ing is a specialist skill requiring training in cataloguing and preservation of the archive material. The National Sound Archive (a department of the British Library) runs training courses in conjunction with The Imperial War Museum Department of Sound Records and The North West Sound Archive. They are members of the International Association of Sound Archives which organizes conferences and publishes a Bulletin. Membership is open to individuals and UK members also receive a Newsletter. They are the best source of current practice and technical information.

2 This, and subsequent references, are to 'Methodology of oral archives' which is chapter 5 of Seldon and Pappworth, 1983, pp. 89–113.

3 As a research assistant and officer on the first project and as senior research officer on two subsequent ones I was involved in these projects between 1971 and 1984. I also taught the Oral History Option for the Social History M.A. between 1977 and 1983. Paul Thompson was director of those three projects and that long association now makes it difficult to distinguish the degree to which I am following his original practices and the degree to which I have developed from them. I would, however, like to acknowledge the major role that Paul Thompson has played in developing oral history. It is difficult to believe that oral history in Britain would have expanded within or without the universities without his commitment, nor that the British Oral History Society would have been so European and international in its outlook, contacts and membership. Any discussion of oral history will be greatly indebted to his practice, and mine more than most. I should state, however, that any views expressed here are solely my own.

4 SPSS – *Statistical Package for the Social Sciences* (McGraw-Hill, Inc., 1st edition 1970) – is designed for easy use by social scientists who are not computer experts. It has been continually updated and improved since the first edition. For an account of *The Systematic Analysis of Life Histories* see reports on the Social Science Research Council's grant HR 7841.

The University of Essex is also the home of the ESRC Data Archive which 'is the largest British repository of accessible computer-readable data relating to social and economic affairs from academic, commercial and government sources'. They hold over 2,500 data sets, many of historical interest, including the data from *Family Life and Work before 1918* discussed here.

5   This table and following information is taken from the final report on *The Family and Community Life of East Anglian Fishermen*, Social Science Research Council, project HR 2656/1, 1974–76; and from Trevor Lummis, *The East Anglian Fishermen: 1880–1914*, Ph.D. thesis, University of Essex, 1981.

6   The relationship of the family and domestic life to occupational and community structures have been further discussed in Trevor Lummis, 'The historical dimension of fatherhood: A case study 1890–1914', in Lorna McKee and Margaret O'Brien, *The Father Figure* (Tavistock Publications Ltd. 1982); and in Lummis: 1985.

7   The percentages given here are from initial print-outs and have been selected as examples of coherence: this may not be sustained in the light of future research.

Chapter 10   Patterned responses

1   Daniel Bertaux, 'L'approche biographique', *Cahiers Internationaux du sociologie*, LXIX, 1980.

2   See Lummis: 1985 for evidence and argument about the importance of these primary childhood relationships for shaping industrial and class attitudes.

3   Franco Ferrarotti, 'On the Autonomy of the Biographical Method', in Daniel Bertaux (ed.), 1981.

4   Emile Durkheim, *The Rules of Sociological Method*, ch. 5.

5   Daniel Bertaux, 'From the Life-History Approach to the Transformation of Sociological Practice', in Bertaux (ed.), 1981, p. 37. It might be noted that in fact others were interviewed, for example, a business broker, in order to complete their understanding of the process by which journeymen bakers raised the finance to become self-employed.

6   Nicole Gagnon, 'On the Analysis of Life Accounts', in Bertaux (ed.), 1981, pp. 24–6.

7   See 'News from Abroad', *Oral History*, **11**, no. 1, p. 16.

8   Daniel Bertaux, 'From the Life-History Approach to the Transformation of Sociological Practice', in Bertaux (ed.), 1981, p. 37.

9   Bertaux, 1981, p. 38.

Chapter 11   Memory

1 Ulric Neisser (ed.), *Memory Observed: Remembering in Natural Contexts* (San Francisco: W. H. Freeman & Company 1982).
2 Seldon and Pappworth, pp. 116–17.
3 I would agree that regular recording of contemporary events by historically informed researchers could provide uniquely useful information to future historians. But it still would not be oral history: it would be a contemporary record with the particular problems of bias which such sources are prey to.
4 Lutz Niethammer, 'Oral history as a channel of communication between workers and historians', in Thompson: 1982.
5 As I understand it this is a position held by the Popular Memory Group at the Birmingham Centre for Contemporary Cultural Studies. See R. Johnson *et al.* (eds.), *Making Histories: Studies in history-writing and politics* (Hutchinson 1982).
6 Audrey Whiting, *Gal Audrey – A Norfolk Childhood* (Ariel Press 1986). The information is from the *Highgate and Hampstead Express*, 17 October 1986, reporter Susie Aitken.
7 Glen Elder, 'History and the Life Course', in Bertaux (ed.), 1981.
8 Louisa Passerini, 'Work Ideology and Consensus under Italian Fascism' in *History Workshop*, **8**, Autumn 1979. She also used published life histories of workers and this may account for some of the 'silences' which attract her attention.
9 Isabelle Bertaux-Wiame, 'The Life History Approach to the Study of Internal Migration', in Bertaux (ed.), 1981.

Chapter 12   Theory

1 Richard Johnson *et al.* (eds.). I refer here to Chapter 6, 'Popular memory: theory, politics, method'. Quotations from pp. 219–20. Although, at times, far removed from practical oral history their article merits the attention of anyone interested in oral evidence and the making of history.
2 Lummis: 1985, p. 6.
3 Peter Friedlander, *The Emergence of a U.A.W Local, 1936–1939* (University of Pittsburgh 1975).
4 Ibid. For all the above quotations.
5 This and other quotations are from the work cited in note 1 above, pp. 205–52.

6   They refer in particular to his *The Edwardians* (Weidenfeld and Nicolson 1975), and *The Voice of the Past* (Oxford University Press 1978).
7   Elsewhere they refer to '. . . the ugly figure of the "historian" (or "sociologist")'. Such comments add a rather unfortunate note to some interesting points.

Chapter 13   Use and purposes

1   Personal recollection of the author.
2   Thompson: 1978, pp. 65–6. He does not accept it as a new method but the re-establishment of an old. It is perhaps a minor quibble but in my view the advent of recording has transformed the evidential status of the spoken word which previously came as 'hearsay' however carefully noted by the historian, whereas now the evidence is always 'original', from the witness, and open to direct use by others.
3   CCCS: 1982, p. 220.
4   CCCS: 1982, pp. 214–15.
5   CCCS: 1982, p. 240.
6   Ken Worpole, 'A ghostly pavement: the political implications of local working-class history', in R. Samuel (ed.), *People's History and Socialist Theory* (Routledge & Kegan Paul 1981).
7   Stephen Yeo, 'The politics of community publications' in R. Samuel: 1981.
8   Studs Terkel, *Hard Times: an Oral History of the Great Depression* (Allen Lane 1970).
9   Michael Frisch, 'Oral History and Hard Times, a Review Essay', *Red Buffalo*, Buffalo, no. 1 & 2, n.d., pp. 217–31.
10   Jerry White, 'Beyond autobiography' in R. Samuel: 1981.
11   CCCS: 1982, p. 245.
12   Frisch, ibid.
13   Peter Burke, 'People's history or total history' in R. Samuel: 1981.
14   Jerry White, ibid. He refers to Peter Townsend's *Poverty in the United Kingdom* (Penguin 1979), pp. 239, 429–30.
15   Age Concern. Help the Aged Education Department. *Recall: a handbook* (Age Concern 1981).
16   Andrew D. Norris and Muhammed Abu El Eilah, 'Reminiscence Groups: a Therapy for both Elderly Patients and their Staff', *Oral History*, **11**, no. 1, Spring 1983, pp. 27–30.

17 Elyse Dodgson, 'From Oral History to Drama' *Oral History*, **12**, no. 2, Autumn 1984, pp. 47–53. The entire volume is on 'History and Community Projects'.

Chapter 14 Conclusion

1 The author's translation.

Bibliography

Books

Bertaux, Daniel (ed.), *Biography and Society* (Sage 1981).

Bogdan, Robert, and Taylor, Steven J., *Introduction to Qualitative Research Methods: a Phenomenological Approach to the Social Sciences* (John Wiley & Sons 1975).

Butterfield, H., *History and Human Relations* (Collins 1951).

Durkheim, Emile, *The Rules of Sociological Method* (Free Press of Glencoe 1950).

Floud, Roderick, *An Introduction to Quantitative Methods for Historians* (Methuen 1973).

Friedlander, Peter, *The Emergence of a U.A.W Local, 1936–1939* (University of Pittsburgh 1975).

Gruneberg, M. M., and Morris, P. (eds.), *Aspects of Memory* (Methuen 1978).

Johnson, Richard, *et al.* (eds.), *Making Histories: Studies in history-writing and politics* (Hutchinson 1982).

Lummis, Trevor, *Occupation and Society: The East Anglian Fishermen 1880–1914)* (Cambridge University Press 1985).

McKee, Lorna and O'Brien, Margaret, *The Father Figure* (Tavistock Publications Ltd 1982).

Neisser, Ulric, (ed.), *Memory Observed: Remembering in Natural Contexts* (San Francisco, W. H. Freeman & Company 1982).

Nie, Norman H., *et al.*, *SPSS: Statistical Package for the Social Sciences* (McGraw-Hill, Inc., 1st edition 1970).

Oppenheim, A. N., *Questionnaire Design and Attitude Measurement* (Heinemann 1966).

Plummer, Ken, *Documents of Life* (George Allen & Unwin 1983). No. 7 of 'Contemporary Social Research Series', General Editor Martin Bulmer.

Samuel, R. (ed.), *People's History and Socialist Theory* (Routledge & Kegan Paul 1981).

Sartre, Jean-Paul, *La Nausée* (Saint-Amand: Folio 1972).

Seldon, Anthony and Pappworth, Joanna, *By Word of Mouth: Elite Oral History* (Methuen 1983).

Terkel, Studs, *Hard Times: an Oral History of the Great Depression* (Allen Lane 1970).

Thompson, Paul, *The Voice of the Past* (Oxford University Press 1978).

Thompson, Paul (ed.), *Our Common History: The Transformation of Europe* (Pluto Press 1978).

Vansina, Jan, (translated by H. M. Wright), *Oral Tradition* (Routledge & Kegan Paul 1965).

Whiting, Audrey, *Gal Audrey – A Norfolk Childhood* (Ariel Press 1986).

Journals

Bertaux, Daniel, 'L'approche biographique', *Cahiers Internationaux du sociologie*, Vol LXIX, 1980.

Frisch, Michael, 'Oral History and Hard Times, a Review Essay', *Red Buffalo*, (Buffalo), no. 1 & 2, n.d.

Haraven, Tamara, K., 'The Search for Generational Memory: Tribal Rites in Industrial Society', *Daedalus*, **107**, no. 4, 1978.

Oral History: The Journal of the Oral History Society, **1**, no. 1, Autumn 1971, and continuing.

Passerini, Louisa, 'Work Ideology and Consensus under Italian Fascism', *History Workshop*, **8**, Autumn 1979.

Thompson, E. P., review of Robert Moore, *Pit-Men, Preachers and Politics*, in *British Journal of Sociology*, **27**, 1976.

Waites, Bernard, *Literature and History*, **5**, 1977.

Other Sources

Gyford, Janet, 'Shop People and their Customers: Witham, Essex, 1900–39', unpublished M.A. Oral History Project, Department of Sociology, University of Essex, 1981.

Lummis, Trevor, with Thompson, Paul, *The final report on the 'Family and Community Life of East Anglian Fishermen'*, Social Science Research Council, HR 2656/1, 1976.

Lummis, Trevor, *The East Anglian Fishermen: 1880–1914*, Ph.D. thesis, University of Essex, 1981.

Thompson, Paul, with Lummis, Trevor, *The final report on the 'Systematic Analysis of Life Histories'*, Social Science Research Council, HR 7841, 1984.

Index